"Leland Ryken is a leading literary scholar of our time and in these pages offers a timeless collection that couldn't be timelier. *The Soul in Paraphrase* presents masterful poems that nourish heart, mind, and soul, along with commentary that is learned, lucid, and inviting. This is a volume that will delight poetry enthusiasts and skeptics alike."

Karen Swallow Prior, author, *On Reading Well: Finding the Good Life through Great Books*

"Some of the most profound devotional exercises—perhaps second only to the reading of Scripture—come from reading and contemplating Christian poetry. But readers today are ill-equipped to do so, knowing poetry only as either greeting-card verse or undecipherable puzzles. In this collection, Leland Ryken, the dean of Christian literary scholars, gives back to contemporary Christians their rich literary heritage. First, he selects works of the highest aesthetic and spiritual quality; and, second, he offers brief commentary that unpacks each poem's meaning, artistry, and theological depths. In showing how poetry is a 'trap for meditation' (as Denis de Rougemont called it), Ryken has given us a resource that will greatly enhance our Christian devotions."

Gene Edward Veith Jr., Professor of Literature Emeritus, Patrick Henry College

"For most modern people, poetry is hard to read and not immediately rewarding. And yet, it is precisely that difficulty and the contemplation that it requires that makes reading poetry such a valuable exercise in a world of distractions. Leland Ryken has produced a volume that will aid Christians, even those not well versed in poetry, in delighting in the rich history of devotional poetry."

O. Alan Noble, Assistant Professor of English, Oklahoma Baptist University; author, *Disruptive Witness*

THE SOUL IN PARAPHRASE

THE SOUL IN PARAPHRASE

A Treasury of Classic Devotional Poems

Leland Ryken, editor

CROSSWAY®

WHEATON, ILLINOIS

Library of Congress Cataloging-in-Publication Data

Names: Ryken, Leland, editor.
Title: The soul in paraphrase: a treasury of classic devotional poems / Leland Ryken, editor.
Other titles: Treasury of classic devotional poems | Devotional poems
Description: Wheaton, Ill.: Crossway, 2018. | Includes bibliographical references and index.
Identifiers: LCCN 2018005833 (print) | LCCN 2018014966 (ebook) | ISBN 9781433558627 (pdf) | ISBN 9781433558634 (mobi) | ISBN 9781433558641 (epub) | ISBN 9781433558610 (hc)
Subjects: LCSH: Spiritual life—Poetry. | Christian poetry, English. | Christian poetry, American. | Religious poetry.
Classification: LCC PN6071.S615 (ebook) | LCC PN6071.S615 S63 2018 (print) | DDC 821.008/03823–dc23
LC record available at https://lccn.loc.gov/2018005833

Crossway is a publishing ministry of Good News Publishers.

RRDS		28	27	26	25	24	23	22	21		
15	14	13	12	11	10	9	8	7	6	5	4	3

for
Margaret and Jeff

Contents

Editor's Introduction

This book is an anthology of the best devotional poetry in English. It begins with the oldest surviving poem in the English language and ends with the modern era. The structure of the book is chronological, but this is a convenience of organization only. Christian poetry is timeless and universal. What the poems in this anthology share with each other is more important than traits arising from when they were written, giving us a new slant on the apostle Paul's formula of "the faith that was once for all delivered" (Jude 3).

No single definition can encompass the genre of devotional poetry, so in the next several paragraphs I will describe it from complementary angles. The first thing to note is that devotional poetry is not in any sense to be equated with so-called inspirational verse of the type that appears on greeting cards. The more I surveyed existing anthologies of "Christian verse" (or a variant), the more disillusioned I became. Most of the material is versified prose. The content is thin and confined, producing what I call "bits and pieces" poetry. The poems in this anthology are substantial in the ways I am about to define. In order to be included in this anthology, poems needed to lend themselves to the kind of literary analysis that I conduct as a professor of literature and writer of literary criticism. If all that a poem lends itself to is mere reading as opposed to analysis and explication, it needs to be judged to be of limited substance.

Most devotional poetry takes specifically spiritual experience for its subject matter, though I will shortly qualify that. While Christian poets are free to take all of life as their subject—and in fact it is highly desirable that as a group they do so—devotional poetry tends to take specifically religious life as its subject. Examples are the person and work of God, conviction and confession of sin, forgiveness, worship of God, and the church calendar with events like Christmas and Easter.

Devotional poetry is also definable by its effect on a reader. If a poem prompts us to think about God and spiritual truth, if it deepens our spiritual insight and experience, and if it awakens a greater love of God and desire to be like him, it has served a devotional purpose. Devotional poetry fixes our thoughts on the spiritual life and inspires us toward excellence in it. To define devotional poetry by its effect is a subjective definition, balancing a more objective definition based on the content of a poem.

Defining devotional poetry by its effect opens the door to a broader field of candidates. Inclusion now depends on how a reader assimilates a poem. If a given reader experiences a poem as defined in the preceding paragraph, it fits the category of devotional poetry for that reader.

We can place this line of thought into the following paradigm for all of literature. Literature as a whole divides itself into three groups, viewed as existing on a continuum.

Literature of Christian Belief	Literature of Common Experience	Literature of Unbelief

On one end of the continuum we find the literature of Christian belief, and on the other end the literature of unbelief. Between these stands a category that can be called the literature of common experience or the literature of clarification (meaning that its chief feature is that it clarifies life). The literature of common experience does not signal a specifically Christian identity but is congruent with Christianity (if it were not, it would belong to the literature of unbelief). A work in this neutral category may have even been written by a Christian.

When Christian readers assimilate such literature in terms of who they are as Christians, the literature can become devotional. We might think of the transaction in terms of imposing a fuller Christian understanding on material that stopped short of such an understanding. Another formula by which to understand the situation is this: if as Christian readers we cannot read X [a specific work belonging to the category of common experience and humanity] without thinking of Y [an aspect of the Christian life], the work has yielded a Christian reading experience.

In this anthology I have included several poems that belong to the category of the poetry of common experience or clarification. I will use my accompanying commentary to show how these poems can be read devotionally. My rationale for including them is twofold: (1) they are too good to bypass in an anthology of my favorite devotional poems, and (2) I want to plant a seed in my readers that can lead them to nudge ideationally neutral literature into their repertoire of Christian reading.

Devotional poems are lyric poems. Lyric poems, in turn, are either (a) meditative and reflective in nature, or (b) emotional and affective. In the first instance, the poet shares more and more of his or her thought process as the poem unfolds. In an affective lyric, we learn more and more about the poet's feelings.

Two English poets of towering stature have provided an additional helpful way of understanding this. John Milton, who turned from a possible ministerial career to his life's calling as a poet when his Puritan convictions prevented him from entering the Anglican Church, was so convinced of the worthiness of poetry that he claimed that the poet's abilities "are of power beside [equal to] the office of a pulpit" to produce good in people and societies. One of these effects, according to Milton, was that poetry can "set the affections [the old word for emotions] in right tune."

To this we can add a similar viewpoint expressed by the nineteenth-century poet William Wordsworth. Wordsworth was of the opinion that "a great poem ought to . . . rectify men's feeling, to give them new compositions of feeling." If we extend this principle to a reflective lyric, we can say that poetry can rectify our thinking as well as our feeling.

Applied to the poems that comprise this anthology, we can read the poems as setting our thoughts and feelings in right tune, and also some of the time correcting them. The same is true when we read the Psalms, and this is a good place to remind ourselves that devotional poetry of the type that appears in this anthology finds its prototype in the Bible.

The poets who composed the poems in this anthology are ministering spirits to us, serving us in ways that they could never have imagined. Their poems have two aspects—form and content. Both are important. Because the content is what expresses the specifically devotional aspect of the poems, it would be possible to overlook the artistry and verbal beauty of their poems.

To overlook the artistry would be a great mistake, for at least three reasons. First, there is no content without the form in which it is expressed, so it is ultimately impossible to disregard the poetic form. Second, it is true of any discourse that beauty and skill of expression increase the impact of what is said, so we need to honor that beauty and skill. Third, beauty matters to God and to poets as they ply their trade as creators made in God's image. For that reason, we need to ensure that beauty also matters to us as readers. The artistic dimension of the poems in this anthology is an important part of the poems' ability to set our thoughts and feelings in right tune, and I have accordingly paid this artistry its due in my explications of the poems.

I am reminded in this regard of a comment that a literary scholar made about Milton's funeral poem entitled "Lycidas," written on the occasion of the death by drowning of a fellow college student. The critic offered the opinion that the beauty of the poem actually consoles, in a spiritual as well as artistic sense. That expresses exactly how I have always experienced the poem. Milton himself said that one of the effects of Christian poetry is that it sets the emotions in right tune, and the verbal beauty and broader artistic effects of a poem are among the qualities that enable that to happen.

A poem that requires more pondering and analysis from us than a poem that requires less is a poem that yields more. In saying that, I am not endorsing obscure poetry but rather poetry that possesses a certain degree of complexity and a multi-layered quality. The more we need to wrestle with a poem's language, structure, and turns of phrase, the more profundity of meaning and richness of experience it will reveal. A perfect example is the four-line medieval poem "Sunset on Calvary" (see page 31). I am sure that some of my readers will be surprised by the quantity of analysis I provide for only four lines, but this is a tribute to (a) how much there is in the poem and (b) how much spiritual devotion is available to us if we unpack the riches.

The main title of this anthology, *The Soul in Paraphrase*, is taken from a poem by George Herbert. In its original context, this epithet is applied to prayer, but it is equally accurate as a description of devotional poetry. To paraphrase something means to put it into our own words. That is what the poets represented in this anthology have done: they have put the spiritual motions of their soul into their own words. In doing so, they have become our representatives, saying what we too want said, only saying it better.

I have taken the liberty of modernizing spelling, capitalizing, and punctuation in all instances where I thought that not doing so would be an obstacle to my readers. Much poetry from bygone centuries was originally published with arbitrary indentations of lines. Usually I have regarded this as an unnecessary impediment to my readers (as it is to me), so I have generally started all lines flush with the left margin.

I have divided my commentary on the poems into two units. I have labeled one of them "notes on selected words." Much of my "close reading" of the poems appears in this unit, which should be regarded as essential rather than optional. Composing this unit has greatly enlarged my understanding of the poems, and I can see belatedly how much I have missed during the past half century by not paying closer attention to every word in a poem. The second unit of analysis is simply "commentary," which I slanted in two directions—general enhancement of a reader's experience of the artistry of a given poem and notes on the specifically devotional aspect of a poem.

The last nine entries in this anthology are pairs of poems on a common theme. These poems are too brief to be an entry by themselves, but they form a perfect combination for devotional thought when paired together.

The subtitle of this anthology calls the collected poems a treasure. That is what they are. They are one of God's greatest gifts to the human race, waiting to be cherished by Christians.

Caedmon's Hymn

CAEDMON (SEVENTH CENTURY)

Now we must praise the Keeper of Heaven's Kingdom,
The might of the Maker and his wisdom,
The work of the Glory-Father, when he of every
    wonder,
The eternal Lord, the beginning established.

He first created for the sons of earth
Heaven as a roof, Holy Creator,
Then middle-earth the Protector of mankind,
Eternal Lord, afterwards made,
The earth for men, the Lord Almighty.

Notes on selected words. *Keeper*: guardian or ruler. *Might*: power. *The Maker*: could also be translated "the Measurer," with architectural overtones. *Wisdom*: "mind-plans" in the original Old English, with the implication of thoughtful purpose and careful planning. *The Glory-Father*: God of glory. *Heaven* [line 6]: the sky. *Middle-earth*: standard term for earth in the Old and Middle English periods.

Commentary. This poem (originally written in Old English and here translated by Leland Ryken) is the oldest surviving poem in the English language. The story of its origin is as famous as the poem. The story was recorded by the Venerable Bede in his *Ecclesiastical History of the*

English People (c. 730). Caedmon was an illiterate farmhand residing at Whitby Abbey in northeast England. Whenever the harp was passed around the dining hall at feasts so residents of the abbey could take turns singing, Caedmon found an excuse to leave the meal early. On one of these occasions, Caedmon went to the barn and fell asleep. In a dream, he heard someone telling him to sing something. Caedmon replied that he did not know how to sing. "Sing about creation," the visitor replied. Thereupon Caedmon sang the song known as "Caedmon's Hymn." The new poetic gift never left Caedmon. English poetry thus began with a miracle of the word.

"Caedmon's Hymn" is an example of the artistic category that we can call "the simple as a form of beauty." Only nine lines long, the poem follows the biblical genre known as the psalm of praise. The content of the praise comes straight from the creation story in Genesis 1. It is an abbreviated account of that story, taking a wide-angle view of God's first creating the entire world and then the earth specifically as a provision for people.

The poem does three things that praise psalms typically do: (1) it begins with a formal call to praise God (the first stanza); (2) it provides a list or catalog of God's praiseworthy acts; and (3) it rounds off the praise with a note of closure in the last line. This simplicity is played off against two pleasing forms of stylistic formality and artistry. First, Caedmon loaded his poem with phrases and clauses that name the same phenomena with different words, a technique influenced by the biblical verse form of parallelism. Second, our spirit is elevated by exalted titles for God, a technique known as epithets. For example, the first epithet in the poem is *the Keeper of Heaven's Kingdom.*

Structurally the poem falls into complementary halves, as signaled by the stanzaic arrangement. The first stanza praises God's sovereignty in creating the entire cosmos, and the epithets for God accordingly stress his transcendence. The second stanza praises God's creative acts on behalf of humankind, as the cosmic imagery of the first stanza gives way to a vocabulary of earth and people.

The Dream of the Rood

ANONYMOUS (POSSIBLY EIGHTH CENTURY)

Listen, I will tell of the best of visions,
which came to me in the middle of the night. . . .
Lying there a long while,
in sorrow I beheld the Savior's tree,
until I heard it utter a sound;
the best of wood began to speak these words:

[The personified cross tells the story of the crucifixion:]

It was long ago—I still remember it—
that I was cut down from the edge of the forest,
ripped up by my roots. Strong enemies seized me there,
made me their spectacle, forced me to bear criminals. . . .
I was raised as a cross; I lifted up a mighty King,
the Lord of heaven; I did not dare to bend.
They pierced me with dark nails; I bear the scars,
the open wounds of hatred. . . .
They mocked us both together. I was drenched with blood
that flowed from that man's side after he had sent forth his
       spirit. . . .

[The personified cross describes its present glory in the world:]

    Now the time has come
when men will honor me far and wide
over the earth and all this glorious creation,
and pray to this beacon. On me the Son of God
suffered for a while. I am therefore glorious now,

and rise under the heavens, able to heal
each one of those who will reverence me. . . .

[The cross entrusts the speaker/dreamer with a task:]

Now I command you, my beloved man,
that you reveal this vision to men;
tell them in word that it is the tree of glory
on which almighty God suffered
for mankind's many sins
and Adam's ancient deeds.
Death he tasted there, yet God rose again
by his great might to help mankind.
He ascended into heaven. He will come again
to this middle-earth to seek mankind
on doomsday. . . .

[The speaker's testimony to the power of the cross:]

Then I prayed to the cross with a happy heart
and great zeal, where I was alone
with little company. My spirit was inspired
for the journey forward. . . .
   It is now my life's hope
that I might seek the tree of victory
alone more than all men,
to honor it well. My desire for that
is much in my mind, and my hope of protection
is fixed on the cross. . . .
   May the Lord be my friend,
he who here on earth suffered
on the hanging-tree for the sins of man.
He ransomed us and gave us life,
a heavenly home. . . .
The Son was victorious in that venture,
mighty and successful, when he came with a multitude,
a great host of souls, into God's kingdom,
the one Ruler almighty, to the joy of angels
and all the saints already in heaven,

dwelling in glory, when their Ruler,
almighty God, came to his rightful homeland.

———❦———

Notes on selected words. *Rood*: cross. *The best of wood*: an epithet denoting the cross. *My beloved man*: the speaker in the poem; the one who received the vision that the poem records. *Adam's ancient deeds*: original sin; the disobedience in the garden and its effects in the world. *Middle-earth*: medieval designation for the earth. *Doomsday*: the judgment day, or last day.

Commentary. This poem was originally written in Old English and is here translated by Leland Ryken. The poem as printed here is excerpted from a longer poem.

The devotional potential of this poem lies in its theme, namely, the power of the cross. Everything in the poem relates to that. The poem draws upon a favorite genre of the Middle Ages known as the dream vision. This genre is prominent in the Bible and in subsequent literary history (with John Bunyan's *The Pilgrim's Progress* being a famous example). In this genre, a speaker or narrator pictures himself as receiving a vision. This is only the external framework; the content of the imagined vision is what the poem is actually about. The opening lines of this poem introduce this visionary framework, as the speaker announces to us that he heard the cross of Christ speak to him in a dream.

After this opening, the poem unfolds in four movements, each one represented briefly in the excerpted version above. First the cross describes the circumstances of Christ's crucifixion; the devotional aspect is that we are led to ponder the physical suffering and torture of Christ's crucifixion. Next the cross asserts that glory has come to it because of the victory that Jesus achieved on the cross. Third, the cross charges the speaker/dreamer with the task of testifying about the cross in the world by declaring the gospel to humankind. The poem then reaches its climax in the concluding section, where the speaker testifies to what the cross means to him in his journey of life. At the very end of this section, the poem draws upon a theological tradition known as *Christus Victor* (Christ triumphant), ending the poem on a note of celebration and triumph.

As we progress through these phases, we are led to ponder the cross of Christ from various angles, including the horror and agony of what Christ endured on the cross and the glory that the cross has embodied throughout history because of what Christ achieved by his death on it. The poem also celebrates the power of the cross to save and give direction to one's life. The final note is doxological, as the speaker celebrates the victorious Christ of the cross.

O What Their Joy and Their Glory Must Be

PETER ABELARD (1079–1142)

O what their joy and their glory must be,
Those endless Sabbaths the blessèd ones see;
Crown for the valiant, to weary ones rest:
God shall be all, and in all ever blest.

What are the Monarch, his court and his throne?
What are the peace and the joy that they own?
O that the blessèd ones, who in it have share,
All that they feel could as fully declare!

Truly, "Jerusalem" name we that shore,
City of peace that brings joy evermore;
Wish and fulfillment are not severed there,
Nor do things prayed for come short of the prayer.

There, where no troubles distraction can bring,
We the sweet anthems of Zion shall sing;
While for thy grace, Lord, their voices of praise
Thy blessèd people eternally raise.

Now, in the meantime, with hearts raised on high,
We for that country must yearn and must sigh,
Seeking Jerusalem, dear native land,
Through our long exile on Babylon's strand.

Low before him with our praises we fall,
Of whom and in whom and through whom are all;
Of whom, the Father; and in whom, the Son;
And through whom, the Spirit, with them ever One.

Notes on selected words. *All that they feel could as fully declare*: the wish is that the blessed saints in heaven could declare their bliss in words as fully as they feel it. *Come short of*: fall short of. *Yearn*: long. *Babylon*: this fallen earthly order of things; the terminology comes from the book of Revelation. *Strand*: shore.

Commentary. This poem was composed in twelfth-century French; the translation by which the English-speaking world knows it was produced by John Mason Neale, a famed nineteenth-century English translator of hymns.

It is doubtless a surprising claim that a major part of a poem's beauty and power can reside in its meter, but occasionally the claim is accurate, as it is here. The usual function of regular meter in a poem is to provide a smooth flow for the words in a poem—to keep the language and content moving onward in regular rhythm. This is what is called the music of poetry. Ordinarily smooth meter is like the air we breathe—essential to the life of a poem but itself unnoticed unless we are abruptly or unpleasantly made aware of an irregular and staccato effect.

Sometimes, however, we are fully aware of the presence of meter as a leading source of our pleasure. The English translation of Abelard's famous poem about heaven sweeps us along with its unusual meter. The customary metrical form for English poetry is called "iambic," and it consists of two-syllable feet (or units) in which an unaccented syllable is followed by an accented one (for example: re-*mark*). However, the poem printed above consists primarily of anapestic feet—three-syllable units comprised of two unaccented syllables followed by an accented syllable (for example: God shall *be*). The effect is to sweep us along at an accelerated pace. Oral reading of the poem will immediately confirm this effect.

The subject of the poem is the joys of heaven—as realized by saints who are already there and anticipated by those who are still in their earthly journey to heaven. The chief strategy in the poem is to awaken our longing for heaven. While the metrical pace of the poem is the chief element in the poem, the imagery plays its part as well. There is a thread of ecstatic vocabulary, with words such as *joy, glory, peace, throne, all,* and *hearts raised on high.* The motif of the endlessness of heavenly joys permeates the poem. Evocative images of transcendence fire our imaginations and longings for heaven too: Sabbath, Jerusalem, Zion. Other deft touches will reveal themselves to anyone who looks at the poem carefully.

C. S. Lewis claimed regarding the term "classic" that once we have developed a taste for it, no other work comes close to being an adequate substitute. This poem surely meets that criterion and is a classic devotional poem.

Canticle of the Sun

St. Francis of Assisi (1184–1226)

Most high, all-powerful, all good, Lord!
All praise is yours, all glory, all honor,
And all blessing.
To you alone, Most High, do they belong.
No mortal lips are worthy
To pronounce your name.

All praise be yours, my Lord, through all that you
    have made,
And first my lord Brother Sun,
Who brings the day; and light you give to us
    through him.
How beautiful is he, how radiant in all his
    splendor!
Of you, Most High, he bears the likeness.

All praise be yours, my Lord, through Sister Moon
    and Stars;
In the heavens you have made them, bright
And precious and fair.

All praise be yours, My Lord, through Brothers
    Wind and Air,
And fair and stormy, all the weather's moods,
By which you cherish all that you have made.

All praise be yours, my Lord, through Sister Water,
So useful, lowly, precious and pure.

All praise be yours, my Lord, through Brother Fire,
Through whom you brighten up the night.
How beautiful is he, how gay! Full of power and
      strength.

All praise be yours, my Lord, through Sister Earth,
      our mother,
Who feeds us in her sovereignty and produces
Various fruits with colored flowers and herbs.

All praise be yours, my Lord, through those who
      grant pardon
For love of you; through those who endure
Sickness and trial.
Happy those who endure in peace,
By you, Most High, they will be crowned.

All praise be yours, my Lord, through Sister Death,
From whose embrace no mortal can escape.
Woe to those who die in mortal sin!
Happy those She finds doing your will!
The second death can do no harm to them.
Praise and bless my Lord, and give him thanks,
And serve him with great humility.

Notes on selected words. *Gay*: brilliant in color. *Mortal sin*: in Catholic theology, a sin that is so serious that it leads to eternal damnation if a person is not absolved of it before death.

Commentary. This version of this medieval poem has been translated by Benen Fahy. The poem is also known by the title "Canticle of the Creatures." It is one of the first works of literature written in the Italian language. St. Francis's communion with the creatures of nature is legendary, and this poem bears the imprint of the poet's everyday life in nature. St. Francis became blind in his early forties (as did English poet John Milton).

This poem has been important through the centuries, especially in musical versions. A familiar paraphrased version of this poem is the hymn "All Creatures of Our Lord and King" (composed by William H. Draper for a children's festival in Leeds, England, and published in the *Public School Hymn Book* in 1919). Elizabeth Goudge's poem "Spring Song" also borrows heavily from the motifs in Francis of Assisi's poem. Finally, in this vein of the dependence of texts upon texts, the dominant element in the format of the poem, a catalog of various elements of nature that are linked to the praise of God, can be found in Psalm 148.

The entire poem is a dramatic address to God, making it a prayer. The genre of the poem is a psalm of praise to God, as the poet consistently ascribes praise to God. Through most of the poem, God is praised for the familiar features of the creation that make up our daily lives in the physical world. The most memorable motif in the enterprise is surely the domestication of natural forces, so that the sun becomes our brother, the moon and stars our sister, and so forth. Just as Psalm 148 moves from the natural world to the human sphere and God's redemption of people as it nears its end, this poem makes that same shift in the last two stanzas.

Sunset on Calvary

ANONYMOUS (DATE UNKNOWN)

Now goes the sun under wood;
I rue, Mary, thy fair face.
Now goes the sun under tree;
I rue, Mary, thy son and thee.

———— ❧ ————

Notes on selected words. *Sun*: a pun, as both *sun* and *son* are in view. *Wood*: the cross. *Rue*: pity. *Fair*: pale or white, and perhaps also beautiful. *Tree*: the cross.

Commentary. "Sunset on Calvary" was originally composed in Middle English and is here translated by Leland Ryken.

This poem is a classic example of two cherished qualities of much poetry: (1) the simple as a form of beauty, and (2) a hidden complexity that is initially concealed by a surface simplicity. The simplicity is what we first absorb: a four-line poem; in the original Middle English possessing two rhyming couplets (*wode* and *rode* [face], *tree* and *thee*; patterns of repetition in lines 1 and 3, and 2 and 4. The religious sentiment too is simple and moving, as the speaker expresses his pity for the mother of Jesus as she witness the crucifixion of her son, and for Jesus himself as he endures the suffering of crucifixion (line 4). The era of the Middle Ages was unsophisticated, and this poem breathes the age's characteristic simple piety.

But this simplicity is tempered by subtle effects. The first such touch appears with the word *sunset* in the title. The word here functions as a metaphor, in at least two senses: (1) the three-hour darkness at the crucifixion was *like* a sunset, and (2) the sadness of the occasion was a sunset mood. By calling the cross *wood* and *tree*, the poet uses a technique known as "metonymy"—naming an object by something closely associated with it instead of naming it directly. The word *sun* is twice used as a play on words in a way that is technically known as "homophone"—words that are pronounced the same but spelled differently and possessing different meanings. The word *sun* refers to both the sun in the sky and to Jesus the Son. This contrast is perpetuated in the claim that the sun/Son went *under* the cross: to picture the sun as going under the cross is an allusion to the three hours of darkness at the crucifixion, and also Jesus the Son went under the cross by carrying it to Calvary and by hanging on it (and thereby being under the uppermost part of it). The reference to Mary's *face* is a "synecdoche"—a figure of speech in which a part stands for the whole.

To sum up, the poem carries a simple devotional feeling on the surface, and then as we trace the complexities of poetic technique, we are led to see more and more meanings related to the crucifixion of Jesus on the cross. Having thus absorbed some of the complexity of the poem, we should return to the simple, obvious impact of the poem. Whereas "The Dream of the Rood" (see page 21) celebrates the power and victory of the cross, this poem expresses its pathos.

I Sing of a Maiden

ANONYMOUS (FIFTEENTH CENTURY)

I sing of a maiden
That is matchless;
King of all kings
To her son she chose.

He came as still
Where his mother was
As dew in April
That falleth on the grass.

He came as still
To his mother's bower
As dew in April
Falleth on the flower.

He came as still
Where his mother lay
As dew in April
That falleth on the branch.

Mother and maiden
Was never anyone but she;
Well may such a lady
God's mother be.

Notes on selected words. *Maiden*: girl, with the connotation of virgin. *Matchless*: "makeless" in the original Middle English, which possesses three simultaneous meanings—mateless [i.e., a virgin], matchless [and therefore unique], and spotless [i.e., a virgin]. *Still*: in this context, silently. *Mother and maiden*: a paradox denoting that Mary was a virgin mother.

Commentary. "I Sing of a Maiden" is a fifteenth-century poem originally composed in Middle English and here translated by Leland Ryken.

Broadly speaking, this is a Christmas poem (also known as nativity poem). Specifically, it leads us imaginatively to relive the annunciation, originally narrated in Luke 1:26–38, especially the climax of that story where Mary tells the angel, "Behold, I am the servant of the Lord; let it be to me according to your word" (v. 38). This famous passage is the basis for the poem's claim in line 4 that Mary "chose" Christ to be her son. In the opening and closing stanzas, the poem celebrates the worthiness of Mary. The middle three stanzas focus on Mary's conception of Jesus and in particular lead us to experience the humanity of Jesus's conception and growth in Mary's womb. These stanzas employ a time-honored literary format known as "threefold repetition."

Setting in this poem is both literal and symbolic. April is the archetypal month of spring (and we might recall that Chaucer, writing at the same time, begins his masterwork *The Canterbury Tales* with the magical line, "When April with its showers sweet"). Spring is the time for new life, and in this poem we are told three times that Christ came to Mary's womb in April. To this we can add the progression in the middle three stanzas from grass to flower to tree branch with its implied buds and blossoms. Perhaps this suggests the growth of the fetus in Mary's womb. The technique in the middle stanzas is borrowed from the ballad genre and is called incremental ("growing") repetition.

Further nuances emerge if we are clued into medieval symbolism. *Dew* was a standard symbol for the Holy Spirit, so the poem makes the theological point that Jesus was conceived by the Holy Spirit. The repeated word *falleth* signals the descent of the Christ child from the transcendent realm down to earth. We are also told three times that the dew fell silently; this is a standard motif in nativity poems, as well as in the familiar Christmas hymn "Silent Night" when we sing "How silently, how silently, the wondrous gift is given." The effect is one of hushed reverence and awe as we contemplate the humble circumstances of the momentous event of the incarnation.

Hand in Hand We Shall Take

ANONYMOUS (FOURTEENTH CENTURY)

Hand in hand we shall take,
And joy and bliss shall we make;
For the devil of hell doth man forsake,
And God's own Son is made our mate.

A child is born in the midst of man,
And in that child there was no sin;
That child is God, that child is man,
And in that child our life began.

Sinful man, be blithe and glad,
For your marriage and peace began
When Christ was born.
Come to Christ; peace is yours;
For you his blood was shed
Who were forlorn.

Sinful man, be blithe and bold,
For heaven is both bought and sold—
Every last foot.
Come to Christ; your peace is told;
For you he gave a hundredfold,
His life for your salvation.

Hand in hand then let us take,
As joy and bliss we make;
For the devil of hell doth man forsake,
And God's own Son is made our mate.

Notes of selected words. *Mate*: the word is "make" in the original text—mate, companion, friend, fellow human. *Blithe*: joyful; light-hearted; free from care. *Marriage*: a reference to believers as the bride of Christ. *Heaven is both bought and sold*: heaven is now readily available to the human race; perhaps an allusion to the parable of the pearl of great value (Matt. 13:44–45), which tells about selling earthly possessions to purchase a pearl that is identified as the kingdom of heaven. *Every last foot*: completely. *A hundredfold*: in full abundance; an allusion to the parable of the sower (Matt. 13:1–9).

Commentary. The translation is by Leland Ryken. Much literature of the Middle Ages breathes a spirit of childlike simplicity, and this Christmas poem is an example. Joining hands in a group as the opening line describes is something that children might do at a party. The celebratory tone of the poem is based on the premise that something new has entered human history, with the result that life can now at last be enjoyed as God intended. The poem celebrates a great advent, with the celebration being enshrined in words such as *joy*, *bliss*, *blithe*, *glad*, and *marriage*.

We do not need to read far in medieval religious poetry to see that the two chief wellsprings of inspiration were the birth of Christ (the nativity) and the death of Jesus (the passion). This poem combines the two events, as the nativity of Christ is firmly paired with his passion. The logic of the poem is based on a back-and-forth rhythm between two motifs. On one side the poet issues a series of commands—to be *blithe* (twice), to be *glad*, to be *bold*, and to *come to Christ* (twice). Interspersed with these commands is a list of reasons why the reader should obey the commands. The poem gives us reasons to be joyful.

We should not allow the childlike quality of the poem to lull us into thinking that the poem is simplistic. Complexity emerges when we ponder the individual claims that are made about the incarnation of Christ. The emphasis is on what the birth and incarnation of Christ have accomplished for people.

Leave Me, O Love, Which Reachest but to Dust

SIR PHILIP SIDNEY (1554–1586)

Leave me, O Love, which reachest but to dust,
And thou, my mind, aspire to higher things;
Grow rich in that which never taketh rust;
Whatever fades but fading pleasure brings.
Draw in thy beams and humble all thy might
To that sweet yoke where lasting freedoms be,
Which breaks the clouds and opens forth the light,
That both doth shine and give us sight to see.
O take fast hold; let that light be thy guide
In this small course which birth draws out to death,
And think how evil becometh him to slide
Who seeketh heav'n, and comes of heavenly breath.
Then farewell, world; thy uttermost I see:
Eternal Love, maintain thy life in me.

⸺⸒⸺

Notes on selected words. *Which reachest but to dust*: (1) which extends to a mere mortal, made of dust (Gen. 2:7); and (2) which ends in death and the grave. *Thy beams*: the light of reason, inasmuch as the speaker is still addressing his mind (line 2). *That sweet yoke*: the yoke of Jesus (see Matt. 11:29–30); there is a pun here based on

Jesus's famous statement, inasmuch as Jesus declared his yoke to be light, and in Sidney's poem the yoke is pictured as producing physical light. *Course*: path or journey. *Becometh*: is appropriate for. *Comes of heavenly breath*: received his origin and life from God. *Uttermost*: full extent. *Eternal Love*: an epithet for God.

Commentary. The highest flowering of lyric poetry in the sixteenth century was the tradition of sonnets about romantic love. The inherited tradition known as courtly love portrayed an adulterous and idolatrous love. This tradition, which of course did not enjoy the sanction of Christianity, is the context of Sidney's sonnet of renunciation. The genre to which the poem belongs is the "palinode"—a retraction, rejection, or renunciation of something that had previously been embraced. In Sidney's handling, the poem becomes an indictment of something more extensive than human love; it also rejects worldly mindedness and false trust in earthly values.

The situation in the poem is a person making a spiritual choice of eternal, divine love over earthly, human love. When placed beside the ultimate value of heaven, earthly love (especially idolatrous love) is something that needs to be repudiated. No poem can be expected to say everything that deserves to be said on a given subject; this poem expresses *part* of the truth about earthly, human love when compared with divine, heavenly love. Sidney's poem is an elaboration of Colossians 3:2—"Set your minds on things that are above, not on things that are on earth."

The structure of this sonnet is dramatic, as the speaker addresses a succession of four "listeners," namely, love (line 1), his mind (lines 2–12), the world (line 13), and Eternal Love or God (line 14). The technical name for these addresses is apostrophe (an address to someone absent as though present and capable of listening) and personification (treating something nonhuman as though it were a person). The line of thought moves back and forth between the act of renouncing something and embracing something in its place (e.g., renouncing earthly love in line 1 is followed by aspiring to higher things in lines 2–4). In addition to these features of sequential structure, this poem is a case study in how poets can organize a lyric poem as a network of contrasts; analyzing the poem to find these contrasts will uncover much of its meaning.

The poetic texture is a mosaic of biblical allusions that are devotionally worth exploring. Here is a beginning list: for line 1, Genesis 3:19; for line 3, Matthew 6:19–20; for line 6, Matthew 11:29–30; for light imagery in the poem, conduct a word search or use a concordance.

Most Glorious Lord of Life

EDMUND SPENSER (1552–1599)

Most glorious Lord of life, that on this day
Didst make thy triumph over death and sin,
And having harrowed hell didst bring away
Captivity thence captive, us to win:
This joyous day, dear Lord, with joy begin,
And grant that we for whom thou diddest die,
Being with thy dear blood clean washed from sin,
May live for ever in felicity.
And that thy love we weighing worthily,
May likewise love thee for the same again,
And for thy sake, that all like dear didst buy,
With love may one another entertain.
So let us love, dear love, like as we ought,
Love is the lesson which the Lord us taught.

Notes on selected words. *This day*: Easter Day or Resurrection Day. *Harrowed hell*: the harrowing (or plowing) of hell was a hugely popular medieval and Renaissance tradition for which there is scant biblical warrant; according to this tradition, after Christ's death and before his resurrection he descended to hell and freed the souls of Old Testament believers. *Didst*: did. *Felicity*: bliss; supreme joy. *Weighing*: pondering. *Worthily*: as it deserves. *Entertain*: consider (as in "entertain a thought").

Commentary. This is a love sonnet unique in the history of that copious genre. It is an Easter Day love poem addressed by Protestant poet Edmund Spenser to his fiancée. As such, it is a climactic moment in the history of the transmutation of the adulterous medieval tradition known as courtly love into the Protestant ideal of wedded romantic love.

The poem is written in an exalted style consisting partly of a long, flowing syntax that sweeps us along. The vocabulary is exalted and rooted in the New Testament. Organizationally, the first twelve lines are a prayer addressed to Christ, and the concluding two lines an admonition addressed by the poet to his beloved. All fourteen lines are a dramatic address to an implied listener. If we break the poem into its four constituent parts corresponding to the conventional divisions of a sonnet, the flow of the poem is as follows. The first four lines, a single subordinate clause, is an exalted invocation to Christ that becomes nothing less than a mini-praise psalm. The second set of four lines (or quatrain) is a prayer that Christ will grant the couple eternal joy or felicity. We should pause to note that although the primary referent of the first person pronouns (*we* and *us*) is the couple, the pronouns actually refer to all believers until the concluding couplet. The third quatrain is a prayer that the recipients of Christ's redemption will be loving both to Christ and all Christians. The last two lines are an exhortation to the speaker himself and his beloved to be a loving couple, modeled on Christ's love.

This flowing structure is matched by a dense poetic texture comprised chiefly of evocative New Testament allusions. Space does not allow for the printing of the biblical passages, so a reader needs to look up the following passages in the New Testament to understand what Spenser is doing: for lines 3–4, Ephesians 4:8–10; for line 7, Revelation 1:5; for line 11, 1 Corinthians 6:20 and 7:23; for line 14, John 15:12. This is only a beginning list, and even where Spenser does not allude to specific passages, the language and sentiments of the poem remind us continuously of the New Testament.

O Gracious Shepherd

HENRY CONSTABLE (1562–1613)

O gracious Shepherd, for thy simple flock
By guileful goats to ravening wolves misled,
Who thine own dear heart's precious blood didst shed,
And lamb-like offered to the butcher's block:
O gracious Shepherd, unremoving rock
Of succor to all such as thither fled,
Respect one of thy flock which followed
These curséd goats, and doth repentant knock,
To be with mercy taken to thy fold.
I know thy grace doth still for wanderers look;
I was a lost sheep once; dear Lord, behold,
And in compassion take me with thy hook.
In one lost sheep new found, thou dost rejoice;
Then know thy sheep, which know his Shepherd's voice.

⎯⎯⎯∞⎯⎯⎯

Notes on selected words. *Guileful*: deceitful. *Succor*: help; assistance; aid. *Hook*: the shepherd's crook, used for rescuing sheep.

Commentary. It is a commonplace that most poems are structured on the principle of theme (a central motif) and variation, but rarely is that principle pursued so single-mindedly as in this poem. The sheep-shepherd metaphor for God and his followers is so recurrent in the

42

Bible that it ranks as a major biblical archetype (recurrent master image). Our first impression of this poem is that the poet perused the shepherd references in the Bible and saw how many he could pack into his fourteen-line sonnet. The poem resembles the answers to a Bible memorization quiz.

When we look closely at the poem's organization, however, we can see that while it is certainly true that the poet put as many Bible passages as possible dealing with God as shepherd into the poem, he did not abandon the poet's obligation to present a coherent and progressive line of thought. The overall unifying element in the poem is the genre of the prayer, as the speaker addresses God from start to finish. We can say that the poem possesses the logic of prayer. The first six lines are an extended address to God, and we should note that the poet uses the epithet (exalted title) *O Gracious Shepherd* twice. This unit is a preliminary meditation on the biblical metaphor of God as a shepherd.

The remainder of the poem is a combination of petitions addressed to God and hints of the speaker's spiritual journey away from God and back to him. The poet makes three petitions, as signaled by the imperative voice of the verb: *respect*, *take*, and *know*. Together these petitions are a prayer for salvation. The intermingled personal narrative is the story of a wayward sheep rescued by the Good Shepherd.

There are too many biblical references in the poem to the pastoral metaphor of God as shepherd to provide an exhaustive list here, but the following at least should be consulted by anyone wishing to master the poem: Psalm 23; Ezekiel 34; Matthew 25:31–33; Luke 15:3–7; and John 10:1–18.

When in Disgrace with Fortune and Men's Eyes

(Sonnet 29)

WILLIAM SHAKESPEARE (1564–1616)

When in disgrace with fortune and men's eyes
I all alone beweep my outcast state,
And trouble deaf heaven with my bootless cries,
And look upon myself, and curse my fate,
Wishing me like to one more rich in hope,
Featured like him, like him with friends possessed,
Desiring this man's art and that man's scope,
With what I most enjoy contented least;
Yet in these thoughts myself almost despising,
Haply I think on thee—and then my state,
Like to the lark at break of day arising,
From sullen earth sings hymns at heaven's gate:
For thy sweet love remembered such wealth brings
That then I scorn to change my state with kings.

———∞———

Notes on selected words. *Men's eyes*: people's view or estimate (of me).
Beweep: weep over; lament. *State*: condition; situation. *Bootless*: inef-
fectual or futile; accomplishing nothing. *Cries*: prayers of anguish and/or

prayers for deliverance; perhaps also weeping. *Featured like him*: having his physical appearance or features. *Art*: skill. *Scope*: range of opportunities. *Haply*: happily; also perchance, or by happenstance. *Sullen*: gloomy.

Commentary. This is the first of several poems included in this anthology that fall into the category of the literature of common experience or the literature of clarification. It stops short of expressing an explicitly Christian perspective, but it is congruent with such a perspective. It is an edifying poem simply on its own terms, and it can be read in a devotional way by adding just a little that the poem stops short of providing.

The universal human experience that Shakespeare here presents is depression and discontent. The theme or interpretive slant is the ability of friendship to rescue a person from that state. The poem is thus a celebration of friendship. The basic contrast is between lines 1–9 (the speaker's bad psychological state before he remembers his friendship with the person addressed in the poem) and lines 10–14 (the psychic transformation that the remembrance of the friend brings). The poem thus turns on the hinge of before and after. The four main units can be formulated as follows: how the speaker feels (lines 1–4), what the speaker wants (lines 5–8), what changes his situation (lines 9–12), and the reason for the change (lines 13–14). The poem's frame of reference is Christian, with references to praying and singing hymns, and even more the two references to heaven ("code language" for God).

The edification of the first nine lines comes from the negative portrayal of the discontented soul and the state of mind that it induces (with such specific negatives as envy and self-pity added to the discontent). Literature gives us two types of examples—negative ones to avoid and positive ones to emulate. The opening movement of this poem belongs to the former category. As we recognize ourselves in the psychological portrait that the first half of the poem paints, an element of confession enters our experience.

Then the poem chronicles a great attitude adjustment. On a human plane, the poem offers friendship as the solution to the problems that the poem has delineated. This is a human value and belongs to the category that the Puritans called the "goods" that God has bestowed on the human race. But we are not limited to this application. The experience of transformation that the poem records, and the language with which it does so (arising at break of day; singing hymns at heaven's gate), invite us to consider other means by which God revives our soul.

That Time of Year Thou Mayest in Me Behold

(Sonnet 73)

WILLIAM SHAKESPEARE (1564–1616)

That time of year thou mayest in me behold
When yellow leaves, or none, or few, do hang
Upon those boughs which shake against the cold,
Bare ruined choirs, where late the sweet birds sang.
In me thou see'st the twilight of such day,
As after sunset fadeth in the west,
Which by-and-by black night doth take away,
Death's second self, that seals up all in rest.
In me thou see'st the glowing of such fire
That on the ashes of his youth doth lie,
As the death-bed whereon it must expire,
Consumed with that which it was nourished by.
This thou perceivest, which makes thy love more
      strong,
To love that well which thou must leave ere long.

Notes on selected words. *That time of year*: autumn. *Bare ruined choirs*: the part of a cathedral or chapel where the choir sits; these choirs are "ruined" because around 1540 King Henry VIII dissolved the monasteries in England, and to this day the English landscape contains dozens of such ruined structures; the bare ruined choirs of the poem are metaphors for trees in late autumn without leaves and songbirds. *Death's second self*: a secondary or metaphoric type of death. *Seals up*: either locking a barn or house for the night, and/or sealing a coffin. *His youth*: the early stages of a personified fire in a fireplace. *Consumed with*: consumed along with the fuel of the fire, and/or consumed or choked by the ashes of the fire as the fuel is used up. *That* (line 14): see my commentary below.

Commentary. This is another poem that does not explicitly signal a Christian frame of reference, but that can be read with Christian meanings and application.

The speaker in the poem is an elderly person contemplating his own aging and approaching death. We infer that he is addressing a young friend. The situation is parallel to the portrait of aging and approaching death found in Ecclesiastes 12, where the speaker paints a haunting metaphoric picture of physical decline in old age as a way of lending urgency to his command to young people to live life to the full "in the days of your youth, before the evil days come and the years draw near of which you will say, 'I have no pleasure in them'" (v. 1). Assimilating Shakespeare's meditation in this way requires that we interpret the last line in the following way: the implied antecedent of *that* is double—not only the speaker whom the friend will soon relinquish, but also youthful beauty and vigor, which the process of aging will inevitably remove. On this reading, the word *leave* means "relinquish" or "give up," which was a common Renaissance usage.

This sonnet is the best-known and quintessential Shakespearean sonnet because it exhibits the features of the English or Shakespearean sonnet in its pure form. Each quatrain (four-line unit) has its own image—autumn, nightfall, and the extinguishing of a fire. Then a two-line couplet makes an application. The three images are metaphors that paint an ever-expanding picture of aging and imminent death.

To meditate on one's mortality has been a long devotional tradition. In the Middle Ages it went by the Latin phrase *memento mori* ("remember death" or "consider that you will die"). As we let the meanings of Shakespeare's metaphors sink in, several devotional applications prove edifying, including the need to accept our mutability and speak dispassionately about it, to embrace earthly life before we become old, and to love those close to us as we see them failing physically.

Let Me Not to the Marriage of True Minds Admit Impediments

(Sonnet 116)

WILLIAM SHAKESPEARE (1564–1616)

Let me not to the marriage of true minds
Admit impediments. Love is not love
Which alters when it alteration finds,
Or bends with the remover to remove.
O no! It is an ever-fixéd mark
That looks on tempests and is never shaken;
It is the star to every wandering bark,
Whose worth's unknown, although his height be
    taken.
Love's not Time's fool, though rosy lips and cheeks
Within his bending sickle's compass come;
Love alters not with his brief hours and weeks,
But bears it out even to the edge of doom.
If this be error and upon me proved,
I never writ, nor no man ever loved.

Notes on selected words. *Marriage*: joining. *True*: faithful. *Admit*: allow to be. *Remover*: a personification with multiple meanings, including physical separation, time (which removes youthful beauty), and death. *Ever-fixèd mark*: a sea mark, meaning a conspicuous object like a lighthouse or cliff observable from the sea. *The star*: the North Star. *Wandering bark*: ship at sea. *Although his height be taken*: sailors determined their position at sea by measuring the altitude of the North Star above the horizon. *His*: Time's. *Bears it out*: endures. *Doom*: the final judgment day. *Writ*: wrote.

Commentary. This poem is Shakespeare's definition of true love and friendship. What the poem asserts about that subject is that true love is permanent and lasts an entire lifetime to the point of death. While there is nothing to prevent our reading the poem as dealing with friendship generally, the inner logic of the poem makes it most natural to interpret it as a comment on the Christian view of marriage as being permanent (for life). Perhaps the greatest relevance of the poem is to a married couple entering the last phases of their married life together (see the references to aging in lines 9–12).

Organizationally, the poem shares a pattern with Psalm 1 in shifting back and forth between positive definition (what true love is, or in Psalm 1 what the godly person does) and negative definition (what the subject of the poem does *not* do). Additionally, the poem is like a framed picture, with the first line and a half introducing the subject and the last two lines serving as a freestanding celebration of the truth of what the poem has asserted. The declaration of the nature of true love forms the central picture.

The Christian cast of the poem consists of two things. One is the picture of true love (especially married love) that emerges, namely, that it is permanent and not subject to the vicissitudes of life that assail it. It is easy to imagine that Shakespeare composed this poem with Song of Solomon 8:6–7 and 1 Corinthians 13 echoing in the chamber of his memory, with their respective assertions that true love is permanent.

The second tip-off that Shakespeare's intentions are Christian is several allusions that appear. The opening line and a half take their language from the Anglican wedding ceremony in the *Book of Common Prayer*: "If any of you know cause, or just impediment, why these two persons should not be joined together in holy matrimony, ye are to declare it." Additionally, the picture in line 12 of the archetypal journey of life ending in the final judgment fits the pattern of Christian eschatology, along the lines of Hebrews 9:27 ("it is appointed for man to die once, and after that comes judgment").

The poem ultimately unfolds its meditative meanings as we unpack the individual images and metaphors.

Poor Soul, the Center of My Sinful Earth

(Sonnet 146)

WILLIAM SHAKESPEARE (1564–1616)

Poor soul, the center of my sinful earth,
[Foiled by] these rebel powers that thee array,
Why dost thou pine within and suffer dearth,
Painting thy outward walls so costly gay?
Why so large cost, having so short a lease,
Dost thou upon thy fading mansion spend?
Shall worms, inheritors of this excess,
Eat up thy charge? Is this thy body's end?
Then soul, live thou upon thy servant's loss,
And let that pine to aggravate thy store;
Buy terms divine in selling hours of dross;
Within be fed, without be rich no more:
So shalt thou feed on Death, that feeds on men,
And, Death once dead, there's no more dying then.

Notes on selected words. *Foiled by*: defeated by; these words are in brackets because the original text is "corrupt" at this point; editions of Shakespeare's sonnets multiply the conjectures for what should appear. *Rebel powers*: the body. *Array*: surround or besiege, and/or clothe. *Pine within*: sigh or suffer inwardly. *Dearth*: famine. *Gay*: brilliantly colored; often applied to clothing. *Cost*: expense. *Inheritors*: eventual possessors (after the body dies and lies buried in the ground). *Charge*: expenditure of money, but also a task that has been entrusted. *End*: goal or purpose, and also destination. *Thy servant's*: the body's. *Let that pine*: let the body starve. *Aggravate thy store*: increase the soul's abundance of resources or treasure. *Terms*: length of time stipulated in a contract or lease. *Divine*: eternal. *Dross*: useless residue left after ore has been refined. *Without*: on the outside.

Commentary. The scholarly consensus is that this sonnet is the most overtly Christian sonnet among the 154 that Shakespeare wrote. The metaphors are numerous and complex, in the manner of Shakespeare's fellow Renaissance poet John Donne, and they require careful unpacking. In fact, the metaphors are what the age called *conceits*—"little ideas" that take on a life of their own and are remembered by themselves, sometimes beyond the context of the poem in which they appear.

The poem belongs to an old poetic genre known as the debate between the soul and the body. In keeping with this dichotomy, the poem is a network of references to soul and body, spiritual and physical, inward and outward (or inside and outside). The entire poem is organized as a dramatic address by the poet or speaker to his soul. The first eight lines are a rebuke to the speaker's soul for dereliction of its duty to curb the claims of the physical body and protect the primacy of the spiritual side of life. The rebuke is phrased as a sequence of scolding questions. The last six lines are a series of commands to the soul to reform its ways. The line of thought in the poem invites comparison with Sir Philip Sidney's sonnet "Leave Me, O Love which Reachest but to Dust" (see page 38).

The only way to uncover all that the poem says is to work our way through the poem slowly and piecemeal, unpacking each metaphor by itself. Four different metaphors are intertwined throughout the poem, and knowing them can serve as a guide to analysis. These metaphors are financial imagery, clothing (lines 2 and 4 only), the architecture of a building (lines 3 and 5 only), and eating. The poem is a veritable collage of biblical echoes and allusions. The following are some starting points for seeing how profoundly biblical and Christian the poem is: Matthew 6:19–21, 28–33; Romans 8:5–14, 19–23; 1 Corinthians 9:27; 15:26, 50–55; 2 Corinthians 4:16–18; 5:1–5; Galatians 5:24; 1 John 2:15–17; Revelation 21:4.

The Quality of Mercy
Is Not Strained

WILLIAM SHAKESPEARE (1564–1616)

The quality of mercy is not strained;
It droppeth as the gentle rain from heaven
Upon the place beneath. It is twice blest;
It blesseth him that gives and him that takes;
'Tis mightiest in the mightiest; it becomes
The thronéd monarch better than his crown:
His throne shows the force of temporal power,
The attribute to awe and majesty,
Wherein doth sit the dread and fear of kings;
But mercy is above this sceptered sway;
It is enthronéd in the hearts of kings;
It is an attribute to God himself;
And earthly power doth then show likest God's
When mercy seasons justice. Therefore, Jew,
Though justice be thy plea, consider this,
That, in the course of justice, none of us
Should see salvation: we do pray for mercy;
And that same prayer doth teach us all to render
The deeds of mercy. I have spoke thus much
To mitigate the justice of thy plea;
Which if thou follow, this strict court of Venice
Must needs give sentence 'gainst the merchant there.

Notes on selected words. *Is not strained*: cannot be forced. *The mightiest*: the most powerful persons in society, especially the king. *Becomes*: is appropriate or fitting. *The attribute to awe and majesty*: the object or symbol that expresses and awakens awe and majesty. *Sceptered sway*: kingly power or influence. *Attribute to God*: quality of God. *Likest*: most similar to. *Seasons*: tempers or softens. *Mitigate*: counteract.

Commentary. This speech uttered by Shakespeare's fictional heroine Portia occurs in the famous trial scene in act 4, scene 1 of *The Merchant of Venice*. The context is that the vengeful Jewish moneylender Shylock has dragged his debtor Antonio into court and is pursuing an attempted murder of him based on a contract that Antonio had signed. Portia, in the guise of a trial lawyer, utters her speech in an attempt to dissuade Shylock from his attempted murder and to persuade him to show mercy instead. Immediately preceding the speech, Shylock had asked scornfully "on what compulsion" he must show mercy as Portia had claimed in the words "then must the Jew be merciful." The opening line of Portia's speech is a reply to that immediate question.

The speech can be read as a freestanding meditation on the nature and desirability of human and divine mercy. The specific genre is known as an "encomium"—a discourse that praises either a general character type (such as the ideal wife in Proverbs 31:10–31) or an abstract quality (such as love in 1 Corinthians 13). Portia's poem follows the familiar motifs of the genre: praise of the subject's qualities and acts, demonstration of the superiority of the subject by contrasting it to its opposite, and urging the reader or listener to emulate the superior qualities of the subject. The devotional aspect of the poem emerges as we contemplate what it says about God's mercy and about human mercy as an overflow from God's mercy.

The poem is a mosaic of New Testament passages (too numerous to chronicle here). Additionally, the poem is a theologically informed statement of the doctrines of works, grace (mercy), and salvation. In fact, the poem summarizes the central thesis of the book of Romans, with its weighing of the relative claims of justice or law and mercy or grace. Just as the book of Romans shows that the law cannot achieve what the human race needs, this speech and the follow-up action in the trial scene show the inadequacy of justice or law and the sufficiency of mercy alone to achieve salvation and goodness.

Yet If His Majesty

ANONYMOUS (DATE UNKNOWN)

Yet if his majesty our sovereign lord,
Should of his own accord
Friendly himself invite,
And say "I'll be your guest to-morrow night,"
How should we stir ourselves, call and command
All hands to work! "Let no man idle stand.

Set me fine Spanish tables in the hall,
See they be fitted all;
Let there be room to eat,
And order taken that there want no meat.
See every sconce and candlestick made bright,
That without tapers they may give a light.

Look to the presence: are the carpets spread,
The dazie o'er the head,
The cushions in the chairs,
And all the candles lighted on the stairs?
Perfume the chambers, and in any case
Let each man give attendance in his place."

Thus if the king were coming would we do,
And 'twere good reason too;
For 'tis a duteous thing
To show all honor to an earthly king,
And after all our travail and our cost,
So he be pleased, to think no labor lost.

But at the coming of the King of Heaven
All's set at six and seven:
We wallow in our sin,
Christ cannot find a chamber in the inn.
We entertain him always like a stranger,
And as at first still lodge him in the manger.

———∞∞———

Notes on selected words. *His majesty our sovereign lord*: a stately epithet [title] for the king of England. *Sconce*: wall-mounted candlestick. *Presence*: royal chamber. *Dazie*: dais or canopy, perhaps over the head table. *Duteous*: dutiful. *Travail*: labor. *Set at six and seven*: in a state of confusion and disarray.

Commentary. This poem was discovered in a seventeenth-century manuscript in the library of Christ Church, a college of Oxford University. The manuscript does not contain an author's name; today it is often ascribed to a composer named Thomas Ford (1580–1648). Some modern anthologies supply "The Stranger" as a title.

The backdrop of this nativity poem is the detail in Luke 2:7 that there was no room in the inn when the time came for Mary to deliver the baby Jesus. Many of the literal details in the birth stories of the Gospels are laden with symbolic overtones. For example, the humble status of Mary and Joseph and the shepherds has been seen as God's consecration of the commonplace. This poem correctly sees a universal principle in the fact that society did not find a place for Jesus on the night of his birth.

To depict this rejection of the worthy one, the poet has constructed a heightened contrast as the organizational pattern of the poem. The first four stanzas create a picture of the frenzied attentiveness that the world gives when a king or dignitary is scheduled to pay a visit, and then contrasts that in the last stanza to the indifference that people show to the divine king of the universe. We experience the last stanza as a supreme irony—a reversal of what should be. It is a stanza that convicts us.

The first four stanzas gain their effect by the detailed portrayal of the interior architecture and household routines in a English palace or great house. This is obviously an insider's description, and part of the pleasure of the poem comes from allowing ourselves to be whisked away in our imagination to what it was like to live in an aristocratic English house. These stanzas catch us up in the excitement of getting a great house ready for a festive celebration. As we read those stanzas, we have no way of knowing that the main point of the poem is spiritual. The excitement of anticipation comes to a sudden halt in the final stanza. The great house is replaced by a barn and manger, and the king of the realm is replaced by an anonymous "stranger." This is an implied metaphor for how the fallen human race and we ourselves fail to give the precedence to Jesus that he deserves. The devotional force of the poem resides in the voice of accusation that we encounter in the final stanza.

Thou Hast Made Me, and Shall Thy Work Decay?

Holy Sonnet 1

JOHN DONNE (1572–1631)

Thou hast made me, and shall thy work decay?
Repair me now, for now mine end doth haste;
I run to death, and death meets me as fast,
And all my pleasures are like yesterday;
I dare not move my dim eyes any way;
Despair behind and death before doth cast
Such terror, and my feebled flesh doth waste
By sin in it, which it towards hell doth weigh.
Only thou art above, and when towards thee
By thy leave I can look, I rise again;
But our old subtle foe so tempteth me,
That not one hour I can myself sustain;
Thy grace may wing me to prevent his art,
And thou like adamant draw mine iron heart.

—————⚬⚬⚬—————

Notes on selected words. *Decay*: fall into corruption. *End*: last days
of earthly life. *Like yesterday*: fleeting; gone. *Feebled*: enfeebled; made
feeble. *Waste*: waste away. *It* [twice in line 8]: the first *it* refers to "my

feebled flesh" in the preceding line, and the second one refers to "sin" earlier in the line. *Weigh*: weigh down, or drag down. *Only*: but. *Old subtle foe*: Satan. *Wing me*: speed me. *Prevent*: thwart or defeat. *Art*: clever designs. *Adamant*: magnetic lodestone.

Commentary. Within Donne's poetic canon are nineteen *Holy Sonnets*, and this is the first one. The poem is a prayer addressed to God. It covers two topics. In the first two lines and last two, the speaker expresses a desire to be drawn to God. Between those two bookends, the speaker describes in detail his despair over his spiritual unworthiness. Donne loves to reverse his train of thought within a poem, and when we come to lines 9–10, it appears that we have reached the turn of thought that the Italian sonnet form (consisting of an octave and sestet) virtually dictates. But the momentary declaration that God will raise him above his sinfulness is dropped in lines 11–12, as the speaker reverts to his defeatist attitude of being totally without resources before God.

The poem is thus primarily a meditation on spiritual unworthiness. It is modeled on the penitential psalms of the Old Testament, with their focus on human sinfulness. The poem is an ever-expanding picture of the speaker's predicament as a series of "bad news" items accumulates. We can discern two aspects to the speaker's desperate plight—a drift toward death and an overwhelming sense of personal sin.

But this sense of defeat is set over against its opposite. Early in the poem (lines 1–2), in the middle (lines 9–10), and at the end (lines 13–14), the speaker turns to thoughts of his God, who can save him from Satan and hell. Overall, we get the picture of the speaker as engaged in a single combat with Satan and as casting himself on God as the only one who can rescue him.

As usual in poetry, image patterns organize the poem and embody the meanings. We can find four main image patterns in the poem: (1) images of decay and decline (beginning with the word *decay* in the opening line); (2) images of height or ascent, associated with God; (3) words related to time and fleetingness, which accentuate the dire state of the speaker; (4) words naming the positive acts of grace that God is able to perform (starting with the word *repair* in line 2).

As Due by Many Titles I Resign

(Holy Sonnet 2)

JOHN DONNE (1572–1631)

As due by many titles I resign
My self to Thee, O God; first I was made
By Thee, and for Thee, and when I was decayed
Thy blood bought that, the which before was
    Thine;
I am Thy son, made with Thy Self to shine,
Thy servant, whose pains Thou hast still repaid,
Thy sheep, thine image, and, till I betrayed
My self, a temple of Thy Spirit divine;
Why doth the devil then usurp on me?
Why doth he steal, nay ravish that's thy right?
Except thou rise and for thine own work fight,
Oh I shall soon despair, when I do see
That thou lovest mankind well, yet wilt not
    choose me,
And Satan hates me, yet is loath to lose me.

Notes on selected words. *Titles*: names and roles (as listed in lines 2–8); perhaps also contracts. *Resign*: submit; perhaps also hand over. *Was decayed*: fell into sin. *Pains*: sins. *Repaid*: redeemed; paid for. *Usurp on me*: take control of me without right. *Ravish*: seize.

Commentary. This poem covers the same territory as Donne's first holy sonnet, being a meditation on the speaker's bondage to Satan and sin, in an awareness of God's sufficiency to rescue him from that bondage. The speaker pictures himself as engaged in a single combat with Satan, and in that helpless plight he casts himself upon God, implicitly appealing to God to enter the fight on his behalf. Corresponding to this contrast between human weakness and divine strength, the poem is structured on the customary pattern of an Italian sonnet—eight lines (the octave) that list the ways in which the speaker belongs to God (a comforting passage of good news), followed by a contrasting sestet (six lines) describing the speaker's bondage to Satan and fear of being an outcast from God. The entire poem is structured as a dramatic address to God.

The opening movement of the speaker's meditation follows the familiar poetic device of the list or catalog. Specifically, the poet lists a series of titles or epithets for himself, yielding an expanding picture of ways in which he belongs to God by right (with the word *title* perhaps carrying an additional connotation of a contract). As these titles accumulate, we get the sense that the speaker is handing over or surrendering himself (resigning himself) to God, from whom he expects certain things as being rightfully his as a follower of God. The titles and roles are a virtual short course in Christian theology, with references to such doctrines as creation, fall, redemption, and immortality. These are a spiritual inventory of what a believer possesses in God, in the mode of the thanksgiving section that appears early in the New Testament epistles.

A counter movement begins with the anguished questions in lines 9–10, with their picture of Satan as a usurper and thief of what rightfully belongs to God. These lines mimic the catalog technique of the first eight lines, giving us a list of what 1 John 3:8 calls "the works of the devil." The speaker's concluding fear in the last three lines is that he will become the archetypal outcast, rejected by both God and Satan.

All of this will fall into place more readily if we picture the biblical psalms of lament as a subtext. They, too, paint a picture of total helplessness, and they, too, are prayers in which the speaker appeals to God to rectify an otherwise hopeless situation.

Like most other poems in this anthology, this sonnet focuses our attention so strongly on the content of the utterance that we can lose sight of the artistry. It is salutary, therefore, to remind ourselves of the rhyme scheme of an Italian sonnet: *abbaabba cddccc*.

Oh My Black Soul

(Holy Sonnet 4)

JOHN DONNE (1572–1631)

Oh my black soul! Now art thou summoned
By sickness, death's herald and champion;
Thou art like a pilgrim, which abroad hath done
Treason, and durst not turn to whence he is fled;
Or like a thief, which till death's doom be read,
Wisheth himself delivered from prison,
But damned and haled to execution,
Wisheth that still he might be imprisoned.
Yet grace, if thou repent, thou canst not lack;
But who shall give thee that grace to begin?
Oh make thy self with holy mourning black,
And red with blushing, as thou art with sin;
Or wash thee in Christ's blood, which hath this might
That being red, it dyes red souls to white.

Notes on selected words. *Herald*: official messenger bringing news. *Champion*: best at winning victories. *Abroad*: away from the pilgrim's native town or country. *Turn*: return. *Whence he is fled*: the place from which he left to go on his pilgrimage. *Haled*: dragged forcibly; compelled to go. *Begin*: start the process of redemption with repentance. *Might*: power.

Commentary. This poem is yet another Donne poem that expresses spiritual terror, and we might well begin to wonder if Donne's spiritual temperament was incorrigibly dark and morbid. It is true that we remember Donne partly as a poet of strain—a tormented soul whose religious experience was wrenched from him. But we can profitably remember two things in addition to this: (1) Donne also wrote poems that chronicle spiritual triumph, and (2) the most numerous category in the Old Testament book of Psalms is the psalm of lament.

The foundation on which Donne built this poem is a meditative genre that was particularly popular in the Middle Ages. It is known as the summons to death (and by extension to God's judgment seat). The speaker's situation is stated in the first two lines, namely, a serious sickness that prompted him to take stock of his spiritual state. The poem is structured as a dramatic address to the speaker's own soul, which is personified (treated as though it were a person) from start to finish. Additionally, the poem follows the prescribed format of the Italian sonnet, with the octave outlining the terrifying state of the speaker's soul and the sestet delineating the ways in which the speaker can avoid his peril of soul.

The first eight lines paint a "bad news" scenario such as we saw in the two previous sonnets by Donne, and by now we sense that this is one of Donne's greatest gifts as a poet. Even more distinctively Donne-like is the brilliance of the metaphors and similes (both based on the principle of comparison and logical connection) that Donne's imagination produced so naturally that we get the impression that he *thought* in metaphor and simile. Our meditative task is to unpack the meanings of these images and comparisons. How is death a herald and champion? In what way is a person on the verge of death like a pilgrim? How is a person facing death like a convicted thief being dragged to execution? And so forth.

The word *yet* at the beginning of line 9 is the familiar turn or *volta* of the Italian sonnet. Its effect is to set in motion a countermovement. The gist of the sestet is that the speaker's situation is not hopeless after all. But the way of escape is not exactly easy, even though it is ascribed to grace rather than human merit. The speaker's soul can be saved if it will repent, and in the last movement of the poem the speaker gives his soul a brief lesson in the stages of repentance.

Color symbolism embodies many of the meanings of this poem. The color images that we need to analyze are black, red, and white. The concluding paradox of red making something white is rooted in Isaiah 1:18 and Revelation 7:14.

This Is My Play's Last Scene

(Holy Sonnet 6)

JOHN DONNE (1572–1631)

This is my play's last scene; here heavens appoint
My pilgrimage's last mile; and my race
Idly, yet quickly run, hath this last pace;
My span's last inch, my minute's latest point;
And gluttonous death will instantly unjoint
My body and soul, and I shall sleep a space;
But my ever-waking part shall see that face,
Whose fear already shakes my every joint.
Then, as my soul to heaven her first seat takes flight,
And earth-born body in the earth shall dwell,
So fall my sins, that all may have their right,
To where they're bred and would press me to hell.
Impute me righteous, thus purged of evil,
For thus I leave the world, the flesh, the devil.

Notes of selected words. *Scene*: scene in a stage play. *Heavens*: God. *Idly*: without proper attentiveness. *Pace*: step. *Span*: unit of distance (literally a hand span), here in the sense of life span. *Point*: mark on a clock, meaning last second. *Unjoint*: disjoint; divide; separate. *A space*: awhile. *Ever-waking part*: the soul, which goes immediately to heaven while the body lies in the grave. *That face*: God's face. *First seat*: first home. *Their right*: their just desert or punishment. *Impute me righteous*: theological terminology meaning "ascribe righteousness to me on the basis of Christ's atonement."

Commentary. This poem is another one in which the speaker contemplates his death. This had been a familiar theme for meditation from the early Christian centuries, where it was known by the Latin phrase *meditatio mortis* ("meditation on death"). Donne turns the subject into high art. This poem is an Italian sonnet, and it is useful to remind ourselves of the conventions of that form. The first eight lines always rhyme *abbaabba*. The sestet is more variable, and in this case consists of the rhyme scheme *cdcdee*.

Additionally, the octave of an Italian sonnet sets forth a problem or crisis, which in this poem is the speaker's imminent death (with the opening line perhaps painting a deathbed scene) and fear of God's judgment. The sestet of an Italian sonnet is expected to solve the problem that has been established, and in this poem the solution is a journey of transition in which the speaker's body remains in the grave and his sins descend to hell as his soul ascends to heaven. The overall movement of the poem is from relinquishing earthly life (lines 1–4) to the moment of death (lines 5–6) to leave-taking and a journey of transition from earth to heaven (lines 7–14).

Some fruitful avenues to meditating on this poem and absorbing its edification include the following. The opening lines give us a string of epithets (titles) for death. They are also filled with terminal imagery (with the word *last* appearing four times) and metaphors that picture the final stage of something—a play, a journey, and a segment of time. The goal of these images is to allow us to experience what it will be like to face the end of life. Additionally, the poem is a mosaic of biblical references—to life as a race, to death as a separation of body and soul, to death as a sleep, to the body as lying in the grave until the final resurrection, to Christ's imputed righteousness as the basis of the salvation of a person's soul. The concluding unholy trinity of the world, the flesh, and the Devil is hinted at in Ephesians 2:1–3 but appears in full-fledged form in Christian creeds such as the Anglican *Book of Common Prayer*, which Donne would have read or recited every day.

At the Round Earth's Imagined Corners

(Holy Sonnet 7)

JOHN DONNE (1572–1631)

At the round earth's imagined corners, blow
Your trumpets, angels, and arise, arise
From death, you numberless infinities
Of souls, and to your scattered bodies go;
All whom the flood did, and fire shall, o'erthrow;
All whom war, dearth, age, agues, tyrannies,
Despair, law, chance hath slain, and you whose eyes
Shall behold God and never taste death's woe.
But let them sleep, Lord, and me mourn a space;
For, if above all these my sins abound,
'Tis late to ask abundance of thy grace
When we are there. Here, on this lowly ground,
Teach me how to repent, for that's as good
As if thou hadst sealed my pardon with thy blood.

———∞———

Notes on selected words. *Infinities*: indefinitely large number. *Scattered bodies*: buried bodies. *Dearth*: famine. *Agues*: diseases. *Shall behold God and never taste death's woe*: will still be living when Christ returns

69

and history ends (1 Thess. 4:17). *Sleep*: remain in the grave. *Mourn*: mourn over one's sins. *A space*: awhile. *Above*: more than. *There*: at the final judgment. *As good as*: as important as; as necessary as. *Hadst*: had.

Commentary. The subject of this famous poem is the urgency of repentance. In the background lie Bible verses such as: "Repent, for the kingdom of heaven is at hand" (Matt. 3:2); "For we must all appear before the judgment seat of Christ, so that each one may receive what is due" (2 Cor. 5:10); "It is appointed for man to die once, and after that comes judgment" (Heb. 9:27). With the final judgment as his premise, Donne devotes the octave to picturing himself present at the last judgment, commanding that it happen right now. The word *but* at the start of line 9 initiates a reversal or recantation, as the speaker asks that the last day be postponed so he can repent. As we follow the thought of the poem, we too are led to contemplate the final judgment in light of our personal sinfulness.

The entire poem follows a dramatic structure in which the speaker addresses a sequence of imagined listeners—the angels, then all the human souls of history, and finally God. A more detailed breakdown of the poem's organization yields the following sequence: the first four lines paint a "commotion scene" in which the angels initiate the last day with trumpet blasts and the resurrected bodies of humans spring from their graves; the next four lines are a crowd scene, with huge numbers of people emerging in our imagination as the poet names categories of people and how they met their deaths; and in the last six lines the speaker takes center stage as a solitary penitent.

Additionally, the poem is based on a central contrast, leading us to contemplate the final judgment from two contrasting viewpoints. First we are led to long for the last day and feel impatient over its delay (lines 1–8). The mood can be summed up in the sentiment "Bring it on—I can't wait." Then it is as though the speaker (and we with him) comes to his senses and realizes that he is a sinner—even a latter day Paul, the chief of sinners (1 Tim. 1:15). If that is the case, the speaker has good reason to want the final judgment delayed so he can properly repent and be forgiven. The contrast is highlighted by the juxtaposition of the words *there* and *here* in line 12. *There* means "at the final judgment"; *here* means "right now, while we still have physical life on earth." When the poet then adds the petition "teach me how to repent," we understand that the poem has been a lesson in repentance, chiefly the urgency of our repenting while we can do so, before we die.

Death, Be Not Proud

(Holy Sonnet 10)

JOHN DONNE (1572–1631)

Death, be not proud, though some have called thee
Mighty and dreadful, for thou art not so;
For those whom thou thinkest thou dost overthrow
Die not, poor Death, nor yet canst thou kill me.
From rest and sleep, which but thy pictures be,
Much pleasure; then from thee much more must flow,
And soonest our best men with thee do go,
Rest of their bones, and soul's delivery.
Thou art slave to fate, chance, kings, and desperate men,
And dost with poison, war, and sickness dwell;
And poppy or charms can make us sleep as well
And better than thy stroke; why swellest thou then?
One short sleep past, we wake eternally,
And death shall be no more; Death, thou shalt die.

Notes on selected words. *Which but thy pictures be*: which produce similar physical effects. *Much pleasure*: there is an implied ellipsis after this phrase, which we should mentally read as "much pleasure *flows*." *Do go*: die. *Why swellest thou*: Why are you puffed up with pride?

Commentary. This poem may be the world's most famous poem on the subject of immortality. The poem is a spirited assertion of the immortality of the soul and an equally spirited put-down of death. The vigor that breathes through the poem springs partly from the way in which the poem refutes the common view of death as being an irresistibly strong enemy who is to be feared. The biblical subtext of the poem is 1 Corinthians 15:55—"O death, where is your victory? O death, where is your sting?" Donne, too, hurls a taunt against a personified death. The poem is structured as a prolonged dramatic address to death, and it is in effect a rebuttal speech in a debate—a refutation of the claim that death is powerful. This devotional poem expresses what it *feels like* to believe in the immortality of the soul.

The poem is organized on the principle of bookends that surround a central part. The poem begins and ends on the same note—by taunting death and declaring its weakness. The middle of this envelope structure consists of a series of reasons why death should not be proud. Working by pairs of lines, here are the variations on the theme of why death should not be proud: death does not actually kill people; it brings pleasure, just as sleep does; virtuous people actually desire death and welcome it as a deliverance; death keeps very bad company and therefore has no reason to boast; death is unnecessary, inasmuch as drugs can produce sleep better than it does. With the accumulation of all this evidence having piled up, the poet asks his climactic question: "Why swellest thou then?" The implied answer to this rhetorical question is that death has no reason whatever to swell with pride.

In this poem, the speaker enters into single combat with death, in a manner that perhaps springs from 1 Corinthians 15:26, which calls death "the last enemy to be destroyed." Other evocative Bible verses and commonplaces also converge in the poem—death as a sleep from which believers arise at the resurrection (Dan. 12:2), death as a welcome deliverance from earthly life and transfer to heaven (Phil. 1:23), and the bold assertion that in the age to come "death shall be no more" (Rev. 21:4).

Spit in My Face, You Jews

(Holy Sonnet 11)

JOHN DONNE (1572–1631)

Spit in my face, you Jews, and pierce my side,
Buffet, and scoff, scourge, and crucify me,
For I have sinned, and sinned, and only he
Who could do no iniquity hath died.
But by my death cannot be satisfied
My sins, which pass the Jews' impiety.
They killed once an inglorious man, but I
Crucify him daily, being now glorified.
Oh let me then his strange love still admire;
Kings pardon, but he bore our punishment;
And Jacob came clothed in vile harsh attire
But to supplant, and with gainful intent;
God clothed himself in vile man's flesh, that so
He might be weak enough to suffer woe.

———⦚———

Notes on selected words. *Buffet*: beat. *Scourge*: whip. *Pass*: surpass.
Inglorious man: a seemingly ordinary human in physical form on earth;
a reference to Jesus during his earthly incarnation. *Being now glorified*:
a reference to Jesus in his glorified state after his resurrection and now

seated in heaven. *Strange*: unusual. *Admire*: marvel at. *Vile*: inferior to the point of being repulsive. *Harsh*: rough to the touch; this line and the next one allude to Jacob's deception of his father, Isaac, as narrated in Genesis 27:1–25.

Commentary. This is an extremely packed poem in which multiple things converge. The key to absorbing the poem is to read it slowly and take time to piece together what happens as the poem unfolds. Because the first two lines situate us in our imaginations at the torturing of Jesus before his crucifixion, we naturally read the poem as a meditation on what is called the passion of Jesus, all the more so because the last two lines also take us in our imagination to the suffering of Jesus during his torture. But the sacrifice of Jesus is only half of what the poem transacts. It is also a meditation on the speaker's spiritual unworthiness.

The sequence of thinking that the poet puts before us unfolds in the following way. First (lines 1–4) the poem commands the Jews who tortured Jesus to torture him instead because he deserves such punishment, whereas Jesus did not. But then the thought occurs to the speaker (lines 5–6) that he cannot bear the penalty of his sins in the way he has proposed because his sins are even worse than the sins of the Jews who crucified Jesus. In what ways are the speaker's sins worse than those of the Jews? Lines 7–8 answer that question. In keeping with the format of the Italian sonnet, the first eight lines (the octave) have thus posed a problem (the speaker's sins) requiring a solution.

The sestet provides the solution to the problem that has been posed, namely, the sacrifice of the incarnate Jesus for the sins of the world. With the self-address of line 9 as the springboard, the speaker develops two contrasts. First the poem contrasts how kings pardon and how Jesus pardons (line 11). The second contrast centers on the patriarch Jacob and the incarnate Jesus. Both Jacob and Jesus took on "vile" clothing (in Jesus's case the metaphoric clothing of human flesh), but they did so for opposite reasons—Jacob to deceive his father Isaac for personal benefit and Jesus in order to provide a sacrifice for the sins of the world. The last line expresses the climactic insight of a poem that has given us food for thought all along—that Jesus deliberately became weak so he could suffer for the sins of humanity. The assertion that God became weak is a climactic paradox, ending the poem on a strong and even shocking note.

Batter My Heart

(Holy Sonnet 14)

JOHN DONNE (1572–1631)

Batter my heart, three-personed God, for you
As yet but knock, breathe, shine, and seek to mend;
That I may rise and stand, o'erthrow me, and bend
Your force to break, blow, burn, and make me new.
I, like an usurped town, to another due,
Labor to admit you, but O, to no end.
Reason, your viceroy in me, me should defend,
But is captived, and proves weak or untrue.
Yet dearly I love you and would be lovéd fain,
But am betrothed unto your enemy.
Divorce me, untie, or break that knot again,
Take me to you, imprison me, for I,
Except you enthrall me, never shall be free,
Nor ever chaste, except you ravish me.

———⚬⚬⚬———

Notes on selected words. *Three-personed*: Triune. *Usurped*: illegally
seized by Satan. *Another*: God. *To no end*: without success. *Viceroy*:
governor of a region; ruler. *Untrue*: disloyal. *Fain*: gladly. *Betrothed*:
married. *Knot*: marriage bond. *Enthrall*: enslave. *Ravish*: seize or rape.

Commentary. This is Donne's most famous holy sonnet. The thought pattern of the poem falls into a three-part arrangement. The first four lines are a petitionary prayer for God to remake the speaker (encapsulated in the final petition in line 4—*make me new*). Lines 5–10 drop the petitionary mode and declare the speaker's current state of spiritual bondage, with the simile *like an usurped town* summing up this movement of the poem. In lines 11–14, the speaker returns to the petitionary mode, with the prayer *take me to you* being a summary of these lines. The poem has a dramatic structure, being a prayer addressed to God. The implied situation is the speaker's bondage to sin and Satan; in his helpless state, he asks God to enter the battle and rescue him, something that he himself cannot achieve. The subject of the poem is bondage to sin, and the theme is that only God can rescue a sinner from that bondage.

Various parts of the poem have their own controlling image pattern, and these do not totally correspond to the thought units noted above. The frame of reference in the first four lines is that of a metal tinker mending and recasting pots and pans. The next four lines are built around the political image of a usurped and captive town. Then the poem progresses to the imagery of romantic love and marriage. In the last three lines, the speaker becomes increasingly desperate and asks God to imprison him and seize or rape him. To read the poem devotionally, we need to analyze what these images say about the spiritual life, specifically about salvation and sanctification. The poem expresses a longing to be free from sin.

We also need to analyze the paradoxes that abound in the poem. To stand, the speaker needs to be overthrown. He cannot be free unless God imprisons him. He will never be pure (*chaste*) unless he is seized or raped by God. Paradoxes require that we resolve what is only an apparent contradiction.

Perhaps the biblical psalm of lament is the model on which the poem is built. Elements of that genre include a plea to God to do more than he is currently doing and an extended portrait of the speaker's helpless situation.

Wilt Thou Love God as He Thee?

(Holy Sonnet 15)

JOHN DONNE (1572–1631)

Wilt thou love God, as he thee? Then digest,
My soul, this wholesome meditation:
How God the Spirit, by angels waited on
In heaven, doth make his Temple in thy breast.
The Father having begot a Son most blest,
And still begetting—for he ne'er begun—
Hath deigned to choose thee by adoption,
Co-heir to his glory, and Sabbath's endless rest.
And as a robbed man, which by search doth find
His stolen stuff sold, must lose or buy it again,
The Son of glory came down, and was slain,
Us whom he had made and Satan stolen, to unbind.
'Twas much, that man was made like God before,
But, that God should be made like man, much more.

Notes on selected words. *Digest*: absorb. *Wholesome*: health-promoting; beneficial. *Waited on*: served or attended to. *Breast*: heart or soul; the spiritual inner self. *Begetting*: a theological and trinitarian term shrouded in mystery; Donne is playing on the terminology that Jesus is the "begotten" Son of the Father. *Deigned*: condescended. *Sabbath's endless rest*: eternal life in heaven. *Much*: very significant.

Commentary. The poet begins this poem by inviting us to share a meditation with him (even though technically the invitation is addressed to the speaker's own soul). The essence of a meditative poem is that the speaker in the poem enacts a process of thinking on a subject. As we read such a poem, we enact the same thought process. In this poem, the poet even defines a devotional purpose for his meditation, namely, to move our soul to love God in the same way that he loves us. As the poem unfolds, we are led to contemplate the love of God in redemption from various angles, much as a prism turned in the sunlight reveals more and more colors. Among other nuances, we can discern that Donne wants us to see Trinitarian references to Father, Holy Spirit, and Son.

As the speaker addresses his soul, and as we correspondingly consider the ideas that he places before us, the meditation progresses through the following sequence: the God of heaven dwells within us by the agency of the Holy Spirit (lines 3–4); the Father adopts us and makes us co-heirs with the Son (lines 5–8); Christ came down from heaven to redeem us (lines 9–12); it is even more staggering to think that in Christ's incarnation God became man than it is to know that at the time of Creation man was made in God's image (Gen. 1:26–27).

This poem illustrates to perfection the three-part organization of most lyric poems. The first two lines introduce the genre (meditative poem), the dramatic situation (a self-address to the poet's soul), the purpose (to increase our love of God), and (by implication) the subject, namely, God's love for his own. The middle (as noted above) gives us variations on the theme of God's love for us. The last two lines are an obvious conclusion to the poem, made all the more decisive by the fact that the two lines rhyme. This concluding couplet is the "punch line" of the entire meditation, and it may even rank as a surprise ending. It is a commonplace in Christian thinking that God made man in his own image. Donne reverses that fact in a thought that is so unexpected that it can be considered a paradox: it is even more noteworthy that in the incarnation God was made in the image of man. The last two lines are an aphorism (a succinct and striking statement that we remember).

A Hymn on the Nativity of My Savior

BEN JONSON (1572–1637)

I sing the birth was born tonight,
The Author both of life and light;
   The angels so did sound it,
And like the ravished shepherds said,
Who saw the light, and were afraid,
Yet searched, and true they found it.

The Son of God, the eternal King,
That did us all salvation bring,
   And freed the soul from danger;
He whom the whole world could not
     take,
The Word, which heaven and earth
     did make,
   Was now laid in a manger.

The Father's wisdom willed it so,
The Son's obedience knew no "No,"
   Both wills were in one stature;
And as that wisdom had decreed,
The Word was now made Flesh indeed,
   And took on Him our nature.

What comfort by Him do we win?
Who made Himself the Prince of sin,
   To make us heirs of glory?

> To see this Babe, all innocence,
> A Martyr born in our defense:
> Can man forget this story?

⸎

Notes on selected words. *Sing*: write about. *The birth was born to-night*: there is an implied ellipsis; if we supply the missing words, the statement reads "the birth *of the one who* was born tonight." *Sound it*: report it. *Like*: in the same way. *Ravished*: overcome with emotion. *Could not take*: could not contain. *Knew no "No"*: would not say "no"; in our common idiom, "did not know how to say 'no.'" *Both wills*: the will of the Father and the will of the Son. *Were in one stature*: were in unity or agreement.

Commentary. In the annals of Christian literature we find a category of works of faith that were penned by someone who was little known for spiritual depth. A contemporary of Shakespeare, Ben Jonson was a secular man of letters (as past ages quaintly designated professional writers). Like virtually every English person of his day, Jonson was Christian in his worldview. Yet his shifting religious allegiances and sometimes unsavory lifestyle show him to be a man of nominal rather than all encompassing Christian faith. The simple piety of his nativity poem (which is what the word *hymn* means in this case) stands out all the more forcibly for coming from an unexpected source.

Jonson was a Renaissance author, and during that era one of the most common subjects for sacred poetry (as the age called it) was the birth of Jesus, usually accompanied by reflection on the theological meaning of the incarnation. Today we would call these poems Christmas poems. Jonson's poem is a conventional Christmas poem that wins us with its apparent simplicity. The governing tone or mood is one of quiet astonishment over the aspects of Christ's birth that the poem celebrates.

Each of the stanzas has its specific duty to perform. After the first two lines announce the Christmas occasion and subject of the poem, the rest of the opening stanza "composes the scene" by imagining

82

key events of Christ's birth—the angels' song, the shepherds' amazement, and the shepherds' finding Jesus in the manger as the angels had prophesied. The second stanza keeps the scene of the birth alive but adds theological reflection about the salvation that came with that birth. The third stanza is a mini-drama in which the Father's wisdom decreed the incarnation, the Son obeyed the decree, and the birth is now the outcome and proof of those things. The final stanza, in conventional meditative form, turns to personal application.

The poem's simplicity is played off against an element of complexity. The rhyme scheme, for example, is not the simple *abab* quatrain but the six-line *aabccb*. The prevailing simplicity of style is balanced by stately epithets (titles) for Jesus. The last stanza catches us by surprise with the epithets "Prince of sin" and "Martyr born in our defense."

Aaron

GEORGE HERBERT (1593–1633)

Holiness on the head,
Light and perfections on the breast,
Harmonious bells below, raising the dead
To lead them unto life and rest:
Thus are true Aarons dressed.

Profaneness in my head,
Defects and darkness in my breast,
A noise of passions ringing me for dead
Unto a place where is no rest:
Poor priest, thus am I dressed.

Only another head
I have, another heart and breast,
Another music, making live, not dead,
Without whom I could have no rest:
In him I am well dressed.

Christ is my only head,
My alone-only heart and breast,
My only music, striking me even dead,
That to the old man I may rest,
And be in him new-dressed.

So, holy in my head,
Perfect and light in my dear breast,
My doctrine tuned by Christ (who is not dead,
But lives in me while I do rest),
Come people; Aaron's dressed.

Notes on selected words. *Below*: on the bottom of Aaron's garment. *Thus*: in this way. *Profaneness*: unholiness; sinfulness. *Noise of passions*: cacophony of sinful feelings. *Old man*: the unredeemed self, apart from conversion to Christ.

Commentary. This poem is a meditation on how a sinful person can become qualified to do God's work in the world. That is the most general level on which the poem can be read, and it is at this level that every reader can resonate with the thought process that the poem enacts. The author of this poem was an Anglican minister, so at a more specific level we should read the poem as a meditation on the minister's calling, especially as it is exercised in church at Sunday worship. The title, "Aaron," hints at this, as the minister becomes a latter day Old Testament priest, standing between the congregation and God. As an extension of this, the entire poem draws upon the imagery of Aaron's garments as described in Exodus 28:2–38.

The poem is constructed on a central contrast. On one side stands human unworthiness to serve as God's representative in the world. On the other side stands the possibility of being God's chosen and worthy servant. It is as though these two are engaged in an ongoing debate that is gradually won by the idea of God's worthiness conferred on sinful humanity.

Along with the surface simplicity of the poem, it also possesses a marvelous complexity. The latter is seen particularly in the unity and symmetry on which the poem is constructed. The corresponding line in every stanza is devoted to a common motif, as follows: (1) the priest's head; (2) the priest's breast or heart; (3) music or sound; (4) rest; (5) the priest's being dressed. This symmetry is highlighted by the way in which the corresponding line in each stanza ends with the same word (*head, breast, dead, rest, dressed*).

Played off against this element of constancy or sameness in each stanza is a thoroughgoing progression as we move from one stanza to the next. The successive stanzas transact the following business: (1) description of Aaron and his garment as described in the Old Testament; (2) a contrasting picture of how the speaker in the poem lacks those same qualities; (3) another counter movement in which the speaker poses a riddle, telling us that he has found a solution to his problem of unworthiness but not yet sharing what that solution is; (4) Christ as the one who can supply what is lacking; (5) resolution (signaled by the word *so*) in which the speaker-minister announces to his flock that he is equipped to be God's minister or servant.

Redemption

GEORGE HERBERT (1593–1633)

Having been tenant long to a rich Lord,
Not thriving, I resolved to be bold
And make a suit unto him, to afford
A new small-rented lease, and cancel the old.
In heaven at his manor I him sought;
They told me there that he was lately gone
About some land which he had dearly bought
Long since on earth, to take possession.
I straight returned, and knowing his great birth,
Sought him accordingly in great resorts,
In cities, theaters, gardens, parks, and courts.
At length I heard a ragged noise and mirth
Of thieves and murderers; there I him espied,
Who straight, "Your suit is granted," said, and died.

⚬⚬⚬

Notes on selected words. *Suit*: formal petition. *Afford*: grant. *Small-rented*: low rent, inasmuch as the speaker/tenant cannot afford the current high rent. *Dearly*: expensively. *Mirth*: derision; jeering. *Espied*: caught sight of.

Commentary. The subject of this sonnet is announced in the title: the poem is about the redemption of the human soul through the atonement of Jesus on the cross. Redemption is presented not as a doctrine but as an experience that we reenact as we read the poem. The poem belongs to the genre of conversion poem. It traces the steps by which Everyman and Everywoman can come to salvation. The controlling metaphor is the lord-tenant relationship, as God is portrayed in the language of a landlord.

Redemption being the subject, the theme or interpretive slant is the mystery of redemption—the way in which it was accomplished in a manner that defies and reverses human expectation. We can see this from the way in which the poem is structured. The central motif is reversal of expectation. A series of false assumptions is discredited as the poem unfolds. It gradually dawns upon us that God achieved his plan of redemption in a surprising way that runs counter to what the human race generally expects.

The poem is cast into a narrative form. It is a quest story in which the speaker searches for a new life. The quest unfolds in four phases, each with a setting that corresponds to the action that transpires within it: the speaker resolves to petition his landlord (lines 1–4, with the statement *I resolved* highlighting the main action); the speaker seeks his Lord in heaven (lines 5–8, with the clause *I him sought* summing up the main action); the speaker seeks his lord in prestigious earthly settings (lines 9–11); the speaker finds his lord at a place of execution (lines 12–14, with the clause *I him espied* serving as a summary).

The last three lines transport us to the crucifixion of Jesus, and the lord's brief utterance is a version of Jesus's statement to the dying thief who requested that Jesus remember him when he comes into his kingdom (Luke 23:42–43). This conclusion is so contrary to the speaker's assumptions throughout the poem that it ranks as a surprise ending. The entire poem consists of biblical allusions that will gradually emerge as we search our memory and conduct a word search to find famous New Testament passages from which Herbert drew.

Prayer

GEORGE HERBERT (1593–1633)

Prayer, the church's banquet, angel's age,
God's breath in man returning to his birth,
The soul in paraphrase, heart in pilgrimage,
The Christian plummet sounding heaven and earth;
Engine against the Almighty, sinner's tower,
Reversèd thunder, Christ-side-piercing spear,
The six-days' world transposing in an hour,
A kind of tune, which all things hear and fear;
Softness, and peace, and joy, and love, and bliss,
Exalted manna, gladness of the best,
Heaven in ordinary, man well dressed,
The milky way, the bird of Paradise,
Church bells beyond the stars heard, the soul's blood,
The land of spices; something understood.

Notes on selected words. *Angels' age*: just as we speak of "the age of Shakespeare" or "the age of Milton," meaning the entire way of life that prevailed back then, the phrase "angels' age" means that prayer enables us to live as angels live—in God's presence, in heaven, in eternity, in praise, and so forth. *In paraphrase*: put into our own words. *Plummet*: a line with a weight on one end dropped over an edge to determine depth. *Engine*: weapon. *The six-days' world*: the ordinary week apart from Sunday, and/or the world that God created in six days—the entire world; everything. *Transposing*: musical term meaning to put into a different key. *In ordinary*: in everyday clothing. *Bird of Paradise*: in this context, a mythical bird that is always in flight and never lands on earth; by extension, therefore, an image of the heavenly. *Land of spices*: paradise; in this context, the celestial paradise.

Commentary. This sonnet is a prolonged meditation on the nature and effects of prayer. More specifically, the poem is an "encomium"— a poem written in praise of a general quality or category. The poem is unique in being without a single main verb (with *hear* and *fear* in line 8 being part of a subordinate clause). Instead of sentences with a subject and verb, Herbert strings together a list of titles or epithets that describe prayer. Most of these epithets are metaphors in which prayer is compared to something else. We can also think of these titles and metaphors as individual definitions of prayer.

The main organizational principle is the list or catalog. To assimilate the meanings of the poem, we need to unpack each epithet and metaphor by itself. At the same time, however, we can discern clusters of imagery and epithets that lend broader units than the individual epithets. The following arrangement emerges: imagery of return, connection, and joining (lines 1–4); military imagery (lines 5–6); musical imagery (lines 7–8); conceptual imagery (words naming abstract qualities; lines 9–10); imagery of transcendence or the heavenly (lines 11–14).

If we read this poem slowly and meditatively, allowing the individual epithets and metaphors to sink in, the effect is like turning a prism in the light. Various dimensions of prayer reveal themselves as the catalog unfolds. The final effect is that of a preparative to prayer, as the poem instills in us a desire to pray.

Virtue

GEORGE HERBERT (1593–1633)

Sweet day, so cool, so calm, so bright,
The bridal of the earth and sky,
The dew shall weep thy fall tonight;
    For thou must die.

Sweet rose, whose hue angry and brave
Bids the rash gazer wipe his eye,
Thy root is ever in its grave,
    And thou must die.

Sweet spring, full of sweet days and roses,
A box where sweets compacted lie,
My music shows ye have your closes,
    And all must die.

Only a sweet and virtuous soul,
Like seasoned timber, never gives;
But though the whole world turn to coal,
    Then chiefly lives.

Notes on selected words. *Bridal*: wedding. *Angry*: red. *Brave*: beautifully dressed. *Sweets*: perfumes (with the implication of fleetingness—all we catch is a whiff of spring). *Closes*: last notes of a song. *Seasoned*: hardened by aging. *Coal*: ashes; cinders (a reference to the last day or day of resurrection; see 2 Pet. 3:10). *Chiefly*: most of all; supremely. *Lives*: in this context, this means "is glorified for eternity in heaven."

Commentary. This is a "vintage" (typical) Herbert poem in having a surface simplicity and an underlying intricacy and abundance of artistry. The subject of the poem is the immortality of the virtuous soul. More specifically, this poem can be viewed as an "encomium"— a poem that praises an abstract quality (virtue). The actual subject of the poem does not appear until the final stanza. Up to that point, the poem is a nature poem that praises the beauty of nature and laments its mutability and inevitable drift toward death. With the fourth stanza we learn that the first stanzas have been a foil (a contrast that sets off and heightens) to the permanence of the virtuous soul. Even though the last stanza is a contrast to the first three stanzas, all four stanzas are joined by the common motif of portraying *the final end* of each item introduced.

Underlying the poem's progression is a process of elimination. Three spokespersons for nature step forward and make a bid for immortality. But one by one they are eliminated, as the final line of each stanza explains (each one must *die*). There is a sense of mounting tension, suddenly released in the final stanza as a quiet exception emerges. Herbert is a master of the quiet ending, and this poem is an example. Each of the first three stanzas is built on a contrast between the first two lines with their picture of natural beauty and the final two lines with their death sentence.

But there is one more triumph of organization in this ostensibly simple poem. The corresponding line in all four sentences serves the same function, as follows: the first line names a conventional poetic subject and declares it *sweet*; the second line describes the announced subject in more detail; the third line delivers a message of doom; the fourth line announces a prophecy—three times of death and once of life.

This poem gives us two for the price of one. The first three stanzas are one of the most beautiful nature poems in the English language. The last stanza is a celebration of the eternal life of a believer in heaven. What we know about George Herbert's life and doctrine lets us know that the *virtuous soul* of the last stanza is the soul redeemed by the blood of Jesus.

The Pulley

GEORGE HERBERT (1593–1633)

When God at first made man,
Having a glass of blessings standing by,
"Let us," said he, "pour on him all we can.
Let the world's riches, which dispersèd lie,
Contract into a span."

So strength first made a way;
Then beauty flowed, then wisdom, honor, pleasure.
When almost all was out, God made a stay,
Perceiving that, alone of all his treasure,
Rest in the bottom lay.

"For if I should," said he,
"Bestow this jewel also on my creature,
He would adore my gifts instead of me,
And rest in Nature, not the God of Nature;
So both should losers be.

"Yet let him keep the rest,
But keep them with repining restlessness;
Let him be rich and weary, that at least,
If goodness lead him not, yet weariness
May toss him to my breast."

Notes on selected words. *Span*: compressed space, based originally on the span of a human hand from the tip of the thumb to the tip of the little finger. *Made a way*: came out. *Stay*: stop. *Both*: God and humankind. *Rest* (line 16): remainder. *Repining*: discontented.

Commentary. This is a simple poem that expresses a profound thought. On one side we have a simple narrative in the form of a creation story. In our imagination we are placed at the creation of the world as narrated in Genesis 1:26–27, where we overhear the Godhead say, "Let us make man. . . . So God created man. . . ." In Herbert's poem too, we overhear God thinking things through as he creates man. The poem's title names an image that does not directly enter the poem but that sums up the main theme of the poem. The poet imagines that God created people with a built-in "pulley" that draws them to God.

The poem is a meditation on a truth that was most memorably expressed by Augustine of Hippo in his famous *Confessions*: "Lord, you have made us for yourself, and our hearts are restless till they rest in you." Herbert's poem elaborates that truth in an imagined story of creation that explains what lies behind the situation that Augustine's famous aphorism encapsulates. In this imagined creation story, we are given the reason why God created people to be restless in the world. The poem expresses a high view of people; their restlessness is in no sense the result of their inferiority but rather of God's supreme value.

One of Herbert's poetic gifts was to domesticate wonder, so that (for example) God's creation of the world is compared to pouring out the contents of a glass in the kitchen, and his worldwide riches are compressed into a hand (*span*). Love of paradox and word play was another of Herbert's favorite techniques. Thus in the last stanza God allows man to *keep the rest*, that is, everything except rest. Again, we usually think of riches bringing rest from toil and anxiety, but the last stanza of this poem gives us the picture of people being *rich and weary*.

The Agony

GEORGE HERBERT (1593–1633)

Philosophers have measured mountains,
Fathomed the depths of the seas, of states, and kings,
Walked with a staff to heaven, and traced fountains:
But there are two vast, spacious things,
The which to measure it doth more behove,
Yet few there are that sound them: Sin and Love.

Who would know Sin, let him repair
Unto mount Olivet; there shall he see
A man so wrung with pains, that all his hair,
His skin, his garments bloody be.
Sin is that press and vice, which forceth pain
To hunt his cruel food through every vein.

Who knows not Love, let him assay
And taste that juice, which on the cross a pike
Did set again abroach, then let him say
If ever he did taste the like.
Love is that liquor sweet and most divine,
Which my God feels as blood; but I, as wine.

Notes on selected words. *Philosophers*: thinkers. *Behove*: require. *Sound them*: probe their depths. *Repair*: go; move. *Mount Olivet*: the Mount of Olives on the outskirts of Jerusalem, at the foot of which is the garden

94

of Gethsemane. *Wrung*: squeezed out. *Press and vice*: machines that squeeze. *Assay*: examine; test. *That juice*: an ambiguous image with two meanings—the blood of Jesus shed on the cross and the wine of communion. *Pike*: spear. *Abroach*: open to let liquid out. *Liquor*: liquid.

Commentary. This poem is a meditation on Christ's passion, specifically his suffering in Gethsemane and his torture on the cross. The implied theological framework is that Christ's suffering and death atoned for our sins, as implied in the picture in the last two lines of the blood of Christ being something that we claim in the sacrament of communion. The interpretive slant of the poem is that the suffering and death of Christ demonstrate the sinfulness of human sin and the love of God.

The opening stanza is an introduction to the eventual theme of the poem. The first four lines employ the technique of fantasy and the imagery of vast space. Philosophers and thinkers do not literally do the things named in these four lines. The general import of these lines is to credit human thought with having discovered great things. But even these accomplishments fall short of understanding two even more *vast and spacious* things, namely, human *sin* and divine *love*. Having named these two spiritual realities, the next two stanzas take them up in sequence.

The second stanza presents sin as the thing that required Jesus to undergo the physical torture and spiritual and psychological agony (as in the poem's title) of Gethsemane. To drive the point of Christ's suffering home, Herbert employs imagery of squeezing a body to such an extreme that blood flows from it. The devotional edification of this stanza is that it leads us to contemplate the suffering of Jesus and the heinousness of our sin that caused that suffering.

The third stanza continues to paint a picture of the bloody death of Jesus, but in this stanza that torture is offered as a picture of God's love, not of human sinfulness as in the previous stanza. The poem moves toward a surprise ending. After the poem has led us to vicariously experience the suffering of Christ's torture and to contemplate the repulsiveness of human sin that caused that suffering, it transports us to the experience of partaking of communion at a church service on Sunday morning. The contrast between the two creates a picture of divine leniency. Sinful humanity escapes the penalty of its sin with something as physically harmless as the communion cup. This is God's love toward sinners. Jesus shed his blood, but the liquid we experience for our sins is the liquid in the communion cup.

Love

GEORGE HERBERT (1593–1633)

Love bade me welcome: yet my soul drew back,
    Guilty of dust and sin.
But quick-eyed Love, observing me grow slack,
    From my first entrance in,
Drew nearer to me, sweetly questioning,
    If I lacked anything.

A guest, I answered, worthy to be here:
    Love said, You shall be he.
I the unkind, ungrateful? Ah my dear,
    I cannot look on thee.
Love took my hand, and smiling did reply,
    Who made the eyes but I?

Truth Lord, but I have marred them: let my shame
    Go where it doth deserve.
And know you not, says Love, who bore the blame?
    My dear, then I will serve.
You must sit down, says Love, and taste my meat:
    So I did sit and eat.

Notes on selected words. *Dust*: the mortal, sinful condition. *Marred*: damaged through human sinfulness.

Commentary. Again we have a poem by George Herbert that possesses a surface simplicity and underlying complexity. At the surface level, this poem takes its situation straight from everyday life—a host inviting a guest to stay for a meal. This host-guest relationship is the controlling image throughout the poem. Within the poem, the guest is the speaker's soul (line 1) and the host is one of God's attributes, namely, his love (line 3). The dialogue is thus conducted by two personified beings.

The poem is structured as a debate and is replete with back-and-forth dialogue and implied gestures. Additionally, there is an implied quest motif, as the host, Love, attempts to persuade a reluctant guest to stay for a meal. The guest's reluctance is based on his awareness of his sinful condition and therefore his unworthiness to be welcomed by God. As the debate unfolds, the guest's resistance is gradually over-whelmed by the insistence of the host (divine Love). The last line sud-denly resolves the tension that has been growing and ranks as one of Hebert's celebrated quiet endings.

All of this is relatively simple, but complexity emerges when we answer the question of what the poem is actually about. It is about three things at the same time. First, this poem is the very last poem in Herbert's volume of devotional poems entitled *The Temple*. It follows poems entitled "Death," "Judgment," and "Heaven." It is obvious that the poem is about God's welcome of the sinner into heaven when his or her earthly life is over. Second, this is loosely a conversion poem that portrays God's welcome of a sinner in the moment of once-for-all repentance and coming to saving faith. Third, George Herbert was an Anglican clergyman for whom the sacraments were very important. We cannot read this poem without seeing in it God's invitation to his com-munion table, and in fact the poem would be at home in any church bulletin on a communion Sunday.

The poem is rooted in several famous Bible passages. The guest's reluctance to accept the invitation of God is based on the reluctance motif in the stories of God's call of Moses (Exodus 4) and Isaiah (Isa. 6:5–8). The final picture of sitting and eating is based on the eschato-logical picture painted in Luke 12:37: "Verily I say unto you, that he [God] shall gird himself, and make them to sit down to meat, and will come forth and serve them" (KJV, the version used by Herbert).

The Twenty-Third Psalm

GEORGE HERBERT (1593–1633)

The God of Love my shepherd is,
　And he that doth me feed;
While he is mine, and I am his,
　What can I want or need?

He leads me to the tender grass,
　Where I both feed and rest;
Then to the streams that gently pass;
　In both I have the best.

Or if I stray, he doth convert
　And bring my mind in frame;
And all this not for my desert,
　But for his holy name.

Yea, in death's shady black abode
　Well may I walk, not fear;
For thou art with me, and thy rod
　To guide, thy staff to bear.

Nay, thou dost make me sit and dine,
　Even in my enemies' sight;
My head with oil, my cup with wine
　Runs over day and night.

Surely thy sweet and wondrous love
　Shall measure all my days;

And as it never shall remove,
So neither shall my praise.

———◉———

Notes on selected words. *Want*: lack. *Convert*: change the direction of; also a theological term meaning "to shift one's allegiance to God." *In frame*: into a well-ordered state. *Bear*: carry. *Measure*: in this context, accompany. *Remove*: move; change location.

Commentary. This poem appears in this anthology as a representative of an important tradition of English poetry known as "the metrical psalms." Especially during the Renaissance (sixteenth and seventeenth centuries), but continuing to the present day, many of the greatest English poets have cast selected Old Testament psalms into the form of English poetry (usually rhymed). For Renaissance poets such as Sir Philip Sidney and John Milton, this exercise was a poetic apprenticeship that they performed early in their careers. Overall, the tradition known as metrical psalms is a voluminous one, and a large part of the tradition consists of psalm paraphrases intended for hymnbooks and singing. As recently as 1995, an anthology was published that contained all 150 psalms rendered into English by twenty-five famous poets from the sixteenth to twentieth centuries.

There is a second reason why it is important to include an example of this tradition in this anthology, namely, to remind us that the original prototypes of Christian devotional poetry are found in the Bible (chiefly, but not only, the Psalms). We need to be aware of this foundation and credit it (even though including biblical poems lies beyond the scope of this anthology).

Metrical psalms exist on a continuum. On one end are paraphrases— translations into English governed by the utilitarian goal of being sung. Even though these psalms are cast into rhyming lines (usually the "hymn tune" rhyming *abab*), the goal is to remain as true to the original text as possible, within the constraints of translation and adaptation to music. On the other end of the continuum are poems governed by the impulse to create original English poetry. The biblical poems remain the basis of the

99

new poem, of course, but the poet feels free to depart from strict adherence to the original in the interests of creating a poem that can stand on its own and is not judged primarily by whether it is an accurate translation of the original. Herbert's rendition of Psalm 23 belongs to this latter category. The wrong way to read such a poem is with a continuous eye on the original Hebrew psalm to see if the English poem is accurate. The right way is to allow our knowledge of the original recede into the background and concentrate on the poem in its own right.

Herbert's poem takes as its subject God's provision for his followers. The controlling metaphor is the sheep-shepherd relationship, but this is not as strictly followed as in the shepherd's psalm of the Bible. The structure is a catalog of the provisions that a shepherd provides for his sheep, and this is understood to be a metaphor for God's provision for people. Read devotionally, this poem fixes our attention on God's provision in our lives and moves us to gratitude and praise as we contemplate that divine providence. At the beginning of the first and last stanzas, the poet accentuates God's love, specifically, as the focus of his meditation and praise. Herbert also personalizes the meditation and adds New Testament references.

The Elixir

GEORGE HERBERT (1593–1633)

Teach me, my God and King,
In all things Thee to see,
And what I do in anything
To do it as for Thee.

Not rudely, as a beast,
To run into an action;
But still to make Thee prepossessed,
And give it his perfection.

A man that looks on glass,
On it may stay his eye;
Or if he pleaseth, through it pass,
And then the heaven espy.

All may of Thee partake:
Nothing can be so mean,
Which with his tincture—"for Thy sake"—
Will not grow bright and clean.

A servant with this clause
Makes drudgery divine:
Who sweeps a room as for Thy laws,
Makes that and the action fine.

This is the famous stone
That turneth all to gold;
For that which God doth touch and own
Cannot for less be told.

Notes of selected words. *Rudely*: unthinkingly; impetuously. *Prepossessed*: owner beforehand. *His* (line 8): God's. *Glass*: the glass of a window. *Stay his eye*: let his gaze rest. *Pass*: look. *Espy*: see from a distance. *All*: everything. *Mean*: humble; lowly. *Tincture*: extract that flavors a food or drink. *This clause*: "for thy sake" (from line 15). *Divine*: holy; godlike. *Fine*: exalted; worthy. *Stone*: the magical stone that turned metal to gold. *Told*: counted; considered; proclaimed.

Commentary. This poem is a meditation on what it takes to live life in a godly manner. It encapsulates the Protestant version of the sacramental life—not the multiplication of images and rituals inside a church, but bringing a divine and heavenly perspective into every aspect of daily life. The second line sounds the keynote, and the rest of the poem imagines what life is like if a person sees God in all things. The poem is structured as a prayer addressed to God, and it expresses the important Reformation doctrines of vocation and work.

The title expresses the main motif with which Herbert works in this poem. Elixir belonged to the fanciful world of medieval alchemy (forerunner of modern chemistry). It was the fantastic substance (sometimes pictured as a stone) that was imagined to have the property of turning base metals into gold. Herbert turns this bit of fantasy into a metaphor in which seeing God in everything is the attitude (the elixir) that will transform all of life from something unfulfilling into something fulfilling. Perhaps 1 Corinthians 10:31 is the subtext that Herbert had in mind as he composed his meditation: "Whatever you do, do all to the glory of God."

The poem unfolds according to the following topical units: a section of petitionary prayer in which the speaker asks God to teach him how to live with God at the center of every action (first two stanzas); an implied analogy—just as a person can look through a windowpane and see the sky, so we can look beyond daily activities and choose to see God in them (stanza 3); statement of the main idea of the poem, using the metaphor of a tincture or flavoring that will make all of life bright if we do everything for God's sake (stanza 4); application to the specimen case of cleaning a room (stanza 5); statement of the central idea of the poem (last stanza).

Easter

GEORGE HERBERT (1593–1633)

I got me flowers to straw thy way;
I got me boughs off many a tree;
But thou wast up by break of day
And broughtest thy sweets along with thee.

The sun arising in the east,
Though he give light, and the East perfume,
If they should offer to contest
With thy arising, they presume.

Can there be any day but this,
Though many suns to shine endeavor?
We count three hundred, but we miss:
There is but one, and that one ever.

Notes on selected words. *Straw*: strew; scatter; spread. *Thou*: Jesus. *Sweets*: decorations or perfumes. *The East*: the Orient. *Contest*: compete. *Presume*: undertake with inappropriate boldness. *Suns*: daily shining of the sun. *Three hundred*: that is, 365, making up a year. *Ever*: eternal.

Commentary. These three stanzas come from a longer poem in which the speaker has summoned his heart and lute to sing of Christ's resurrection. They form a brief "song" that is a rapturous celebration of the glory of the annual resurrection day.

Much devotional poetry employs a technique that goes back to medieval traditions of contemplation, namely, to begin a poem by "composing the scene" (as devotional manuals called it). This means imagining oneself present at an event, usually an event narrated in the Bible but in this case the usual Easter Day rituals in a small rural town in England. Herbert situates himself in his native town of Bemerton (we infer), which was (and still is) surrounded by farmland and pastures. The actions that the speaker performs in the first two lines are celebratory ones, reminiscent of folk holidays like May Day when greenery was brought in from the woods into people's houses. Line 2 "goes one better" than that by also evoking the celebration of the crowds at the Triumphal Entry of Jesus into Jerusalem.

The next two lines immediately undercut the speaker's self-congratulatory sense of "doing it right" on Easter morning. The poet imagines Jesus as being already present on resurrection morning, bringing his own festive decorations with him. The implied point is that the resurrection of Jesus is greater than any commemoration that we can orchestrate.

The entire rest of the poem is an elaboration of this idea, as the resurrection of Jesus is declared to be so superior that it renders other things superfluous or inferior. For example, the sun rising in the East and perfumes imported from the Orient are presumptuous if they think that can compete in glory with the resurrection of Jesus. Similarly, no number of sunrises can match the splendor of Easter Day, and even though we calculate 365 days in a year (rounded off to *three hundred*), Easter Day is so important as to completely supplant all the other days. The poem thus uses hyperbole to assert the supreme value of Easter Day and Christ's resurrection from the dead.

The Collar

GEORGE HERBERT (1593–1633)

I struck the board, and cried, "No more;
               I will abroad!
What? Shall I ever sigh and pine?
My lines and life are free, free as the road,
Loose as the wind, as large as store.
        Shall I be still in suit?
Have I no harvest but a thorn
To let me blood, and not restore
What I have lost with cordial fruit?
        Sure there was wine
Before my sighs did dry it; there was corn
   Before my tears did drown it.
     Is the year only lost to me?
       Have I no bays to crown it,
No flowers, no garlands gay? All blasted?
              All wasted?
Not so, my heart; but there is fruit,
   And thou hast hands.
Recover all thy sigh-blown age
On double pleasures: leave thy cold dispute
Of what is fit and not. Forsake thy cage,
     Thy rope of sands,
Which petty thoughts have made, and made to thee
Good cable, to enforce and draw,
     And be thy law,
While thou didst wink and wouldst not see.
     Away! Take heed;
     I will abroad.

> Call in thy death's-head there; tie up thy fears;
>   He that forbears
>   To suit and serve his need
>   Deserves his load."
> But as I raved and grew more fierce and wild
>   At every word,
> Methought I heard one calling, *Child!*
>   And I replied *My Lord*.

Notes on selected words. *Board*: kitchen table. *Abroad*: leave; go abroad. *Pine*: wither away; languish. *Lines*: condition. *Store*: storehouse; granary. *Suit*: service. *Let me blood*: cause me to bleed. *Cordial*: life-restoring. *Bays*: crown made of laurel leaves. *Gay*: colorful; festive. *Sigh-blown*: dominated by sighs. *Good*: strong. *Wink*: close one's eyes. *Take heed*: beware of me; get out of my way. *Methought*: I thought.

Commentary. This is George Herbert's major lyric in its length and complexity. It requires a reader's best powers of concentration and analysis. Yet the last four lines have a winsome simplicity and are Herbert's most famous quiet ending. The controlling metaphor is the lord-tenant relationship, with the speaker quickly emerging as a discontented farmer who is in a state of rebellion against renting his farm from his landlord. The style is colloquial, filled with the vigor of everyday language as the speaker addresses himself.

The conversation between the speaker and himself follows the flow of thought and feeling as it goes on inside the speaker's mind. The frequent questions that the speaker asks and the commands that he utters capture the rebellious thoughts and feelings that govern his meandering line of thinking. Of course this is metaphoric of a soul in rebellion against God and his rules for living. The overall organization is an arc of increasing rage, as the speaker first takes stock of his current situation and rebels against it, and then embraces a vaguely conceived alternative life. In the last four lines, the speaker suddenly reverses himself and submits to the voice of his lord (God) calling him.

On this overall action of rebellion and return Herbert composes a rich and sometimes difficult poetic texture. Herbert belonged to the seventeenth-century "school" of poetry known as the metaphysical poets, and they wrote poetry that is "metaphorically strong," meaning that metaphors and similes and analogies embody much of the meaning of their poems. To master this poem requires that we spend time on the individual images and comparisons, unpacking the meanings of each one individually. Even the title captures the qualities of metaphor and pun. The collar is first of all the harness or halter worn by a horse—an image of imposed discipline that was a frequent metaphor for living a disciplined Christian life. But there are two puns on that word as well—"choler," meaning rage, and "caller," in keeping with the voice of *one calling* on which the whole poem turns.

To read the poem devotionally, we need to meditate on the nature of discontent in the Christian life that the poem places before us, the temptation that we might feel part of the time to reject the life of discipline and embrace a life of "freedom," and a concluding awareness that submission to God is the Christian's rightful place of security. At the end of the poem the speaker returns home as a child who has come to his spiritual senses.

Sunday

GEORGE HERBERT (1593–1633)

O day most calm, most bright,
The fruit of this, the next world's bud,
The endorsement of supreme delight,
Writ by a friend, and with his blood;
The couch of time; care's balm and bay:
The week were dark, but for thy light:
Thy torch doth show the way.

The other days and thou
Make up one man; whose face thou art,
Knocking at heaven with thy brow:
The work-days are the back-part;
The burden of the week lies there,
Making the whole to stoop and bow,
Till thy release appear. . . .

Sundays the pillars are,
On which heaven's palace archèd lies:
The other days fill up the spare
And hollow room with vanities.
They are the fruitful beds and borders
In God's rich garden: that is bare,
Which parts their ranks and orders.

The Sundays of man's life,
Threaded together on time's string,
Make bracelets to adorn the wife
Of the eternal glorious King.

On Sunday heaven's gate stands ope;
Blessings are plentiful and rife,
More plentiful than hope.

This day my Savior rose,
And did enclose this light for his:
That, as each beast his manger knows,
Man might not of his fodder miss.
Christ hath took in this piece of ground,
And made a garden there for those
Who want herbs for their wound. . . .

Thou art a day of mirth:
And where the weekdays trail on ground,
Thy flight is higher, as thy birth.
O let me take thee at the bound,
Leaping with thee from seven to seven,
Till that we both, being tossed from earth,
Fly hand in hand to heaven!

———— ∞ ————

Notes on selected words. *This* [line 2]: this world. *Bud*: the metaphoric meaning is that Sunday is a small foreshadowing of what heaven will be like. *Endorsement of*: giving approval to. *Writ*: written. *A friend*: Jesus. *Couch*: resting place. *Bay*: bay oil with medicinal properties; intended to be paired with the earlier word *balm*. *But*: except. *Vanities*: empty things. *They*: Sundays, the subject introduced at the start of this stanza. *That*: the other six days of the week. *Parts*: divides; the reference is to the garden pathways that divide the flower beds (called *ranks and orders*); we can infer that the barren pathways represent the weekdays. *Ope*: open. *Rife*: full; abundant. *Than hope*: than hoped for or expected. *Want*: need. *From seven to seven*: from week to week.

Commentary. This poem resembles Herbert's sonnet on prayer (earlier in this anthology) in three ways: it is a list of descriptors of the subject;

most of the descriptions are metaphors; and the list not only describes the subject but praises it. The verse form, rhyming *ababcac*, adds a pleasant artistry to the poem.

Two organizational patterns are at work. One is the succession of stanzas. The stanzas are not unified by just one image, nor do they have a strict topical unity, but the individual stanzas nonetheless strike us as dealing with a cluster of related images under a loosely unifying umbrella. The stanzas *feel* like a unity, and as we begin a stanza, we sense that the thought has now taken a new direction. The second principle of organization consists of an underlying contrast between the superiority of Sunday and the inferiority of the rest of the week. This is not rigidly followed, but we are continuously aware that Sunday is being elevated above the other six days.

The concept of theme and variation binds the foregoing considerations together. The unifying theme is the supreme value of Sunday as a gift from God. The variations are the specific ways in which Sunday is presented as the best day. The purpose of literature is to raise our awareness about life, and as we ponder each stanza with its metaphors, we come to see Sunday more clearly and value it more.

He Bore Our Griefs

JACOBUS REVIUS (1586–1658)

No, it was not the Jews who crucified,
Nor who betrayed you in the judgment place,
Nor who, Lord Jesus, spat into your face,
Nor who with buffets struck you as you died.
No, it was not the soldiers fisted bold
Who lifted up the hammer and the nail,
Or raised the cursèd cross on Calvary's hill,
Or, gambling, tossed the dice to win your robe.
I am the one, O Lord, who brought you there,
I am the heavy cross you had to bear,
I am the rope that bound you to the tree,
The whip, the nail, the hammer, and the spear,
The blood-stained crown of thorns you had to wear:
It was my sin, alas, it was for me.

———⊶⊷———

Notes on selected words. *Spat*: spit. *Buffets*: blows with the hand.

Commentary. Jacobus Revius was a Dutch poet who wrote at the same time as the English poets John Donne and George Herbert. Like Donne and Herbert, he wrote in a style known to literary scholars as metaphysical. The sonnet printed here (as translated by Henrietta Ten Harmsel) is his most famous poem.

The poem is a confession of guilt addressed directly to Christ in a prayer-like stance. It is an Italian sonnet in which the octave rehearses what is *not* true about Christ's crucifixion, namely, that the Jews were responsible for the execution. The sestet then states the positive counterpart of that by declaring what *is* true about the crucifixion, namely, that the speaker is the one responsible for it. Like many other poems in the metaphysical tradition of poetry, the poem secures its effect by paradox and surprise. Everyone knows that it was the Jews who conspired against Jesus and killed him, but that is only the externality of the matter. Jesus's death was an atoning substitutionary death for sinners, so that every sinner for whom Christ died can be said to be the one who killed him. In this poem, Revius does what his contemporary Dutch artist Rembrandt did when he painted himself at the foot of the cross as Christ is raised on it (in *Raising of the Cross*).

The biblical foundation for Revius's poem is Isaiah 53, with such lines as "surely he has borne our griefs" (v. 4) and "he was pierced for our transgressions; he was crushed for our iniquities" (v. 5). Within that theological framework, the poet "composes the scene" by imagining the details of the crucifixion as recorded in the Gospels. There is a division of duties between the octave, in which the speaker pictures himself among those who tortured Christ, and the sestet, where the speaker identifies himself with the instruments of torture. The last line is the climax of the poem and states directly the basis for the speaker's claims throughout the poem, namely, that it was his sin that caused the crucifixion.

His Savior's Words, Going to the Cross

ROBERT HERRICK (1591–1674)

Have, have ye no regard, all ye
Who pass this way, to pity me,
Who am a man of misery!
A man both bruised and broke,
    and one
Who suffers not here for mine own,
But for my friends' transgression!
Ah! Sion's Daughters, do not fear
The cross, the cords, the nails, the spear,
The myrrh, the gall, the vinegar:
For Christ, your loving Savior, hath
Drunk up the wine of God's fierce wrath;
Only, there's left a little froth,
Less for to taste, than for to show,
What bitter cups had been your due,
Had He not drank them up for you.

Notes on selected words. *Sion*: Zion, meaning Jerusalem. *Sion's daughters*: the metaphoric epithet "Daughters of Jerusalem" (or variants thereof) is a biblical designation that broadly means "the people of

God." *Cords*: whips designed to inflict torture. *Gall*: bitter liquid. *Wrath*: anger. *Froth*: foam formed on top of a liquid. *Show*: demonstrate. *Drank*: drunk.

Commentary. This ostensibly simple poem holds an abundance of devotional richness. The rhyme scheme of triplets (three consecutive rhyming sounds) reinforces the accessibility of the poem to any humble spirit. As the title signals, the poem is an imagined speech by Jesus in the suffering of his passion. His words are addressed to the metaphoric daughters of Jerusalem, meaning all who believe in Jesus as their Savior. The main message of the dying Savior is that he has suffered the penalty of human sins as a sacrifice. As we unpack the individual images, we are led to feel from a variety of angles the suffering caused by human sinfulness, and correspondingly how much Jesus endured. Nearly every line reminds us of some biblical passage or image.

The first nine lines draw upon a longstanding meditative tradition known as "composing the scene," by which is meant imagining oneself present at an event in the Bible, in this case the crucifixion. In just two packed lines in the middle of the poem, Herrick reminds us of nearly the whole story of Jesus's torture and crucifixion. A main design of the first third of the poem is to evoke our pity and compassion for the suffering Savior. Isaiah 53, the song of the suffering servant, is the subtext for lines 4–6, with their imagery of bruising, suffering, transgression, and substitution. Having aroused a sense of terror, the poet then allays that terror by a calm assertion from a loving Christ that he has satisfied God's wrath against sin.

The final movement of the poem springs a surprise ending on us. According to familiar theology, reinforced by the poem up to this point, Jesus fully satisfied the penalty of all sin committed by those who believe in him as Savior. The poem does not dispute that, but it offers an original insight by tapping into the universal human experience that we all know firsthand of bringing misery on ourselves by our sinful actions. According to the poem, these relatively small sufferings can give us an insight into the supreme suffering of Jesus for our sins in his role of substitute (*for you*).

His Litany to the Holy Spirit

ROBERT HERRICK (1591–1674)

In the hour of my distress,
When temptations me oppress,
And when I my sins confess,
  Sweet Spirit, comfort me!

When I lie within my bed,
Sick in heart, and sick in head,
And with doubts discomforted,
  Sweet Spirit, comfort me!

When the house doth sigh and weep,
And the world is drowned in sleep,
Yet mine eyes the watch do keep,
  Sweet Spirit, comfort me! . . .

When the passing-bell doth toll,
And the furies in a shoal
Come to fright a parting soul,
  Sweet Spirit, comfort me!

When the tapers now burn blue,
And the comforters are few,
And that number more than true,
  Sweet Spirit, comfort me!

When the priest his last hath prayed,
And I nod to what is said,

Because my speech is now decayed,
    Sweet Spirit, comfort me!

When, God knows, I am tossed about
Either with despair, or doubt;
Yet, before the glass be out,
    Sweet Spirit, comfort me!

When the tempter me pursueth
With the sins of all my youth,
And half damns me with untruth,
    Sweet Spirit, comfort me!

When the flames and hellish cries
Fright mine ears, and fright mine eyes,
And all terrors me surprise,
    Sweet Spirit, comfort me!

When the Judgment is revealed,
And that opened which was sealed;
When to Thee I have appealed,
    Sweet Spirit, comfort me!

Notes on selected words. *Litany*: a prayer consisting of a series of pe-
titions. *Discomforted*: disturbed; made uncomfortable. *Passing-bell*:
bell rung to announce a death. *Furies in a shoal*: demons together in a
group or pack. *Tapers*: slender candles. *That number more than true*:
possibly a reference to *few* in the preceding line, with the meaning
that even the count of "few" is too high. *Decayed*: inaudible. *Glass*:
hourglass (a timepiece). *The tempter*: Satan. *The Judgment*: God's final
judgment on the last day. *That opened which was sealed*: God's book
of judgment for people, to be unsealed at the last day.

Commentary. The first thing we need to know about this poem (here
excerpted) is that the implied situation is that the speaker is on his

deathbed (a situation duplicated in several other poems in this anthology). The poem is the speaker's imagined last prayer to God, and in an original twist he addresses his petitions to the third person of the Trinity, who is known as the Comforter. Every stanza ends with the same refrain line, which anchors the speaker's prayer to the Holy Spirit in his role as comforter and underscores his need for comfort in the ultimate extremity, death. As we move through the poem, various features of the speaker's dire situation are rehearsed in our presence. A moving picture of ultimate helplessness unfolds before us. The thing that remains constant through this progression is the speaker's need for the comfort of the Holy Spirit in all of his extremities.

In the background of this poem is a very old meditative tradition of contemplating one's own death. Poets have been particularly adept at imagining the moments leading to physical death. The spiritual benefit of such contemplation lies in its realism. We know abstractly that we will die, but abstractions generally do not have the impact they should. The imagination rescues us from the impotence of abstraction—and from the evasion of reality that living in a realm of abstractions can easily produce. Once we have felt the vicarious reality of our own physical death by reading Herrick's deathbed poem, we are also led to ponder what our consolation will be when we live through the actuality of death. Herrick's poem offers the comfort of the Holy Spirit. The poem is a "dress rehearsal" of our own death.

The first three lines of each stanza employ a single rhyming sound, and this, combined with the shortness of the lines, imposes a simplicity on Herrick's imagined enactment of his death. Freed from the need to engage in detailed analysis, we can allow each snapshot to register with us, and then contemplate how the comfort of the Holy Spirit will be a defense against what the speaker feels as an attack.

On Time

JOHN MILTON (1608–1674)

Fly envious Time, till thou run out thy race;
Call on the lazy leaden-stepping hours,
Whose speed is but the heavy Plummets pace;
And glut thy self with what thy womb devours,
Which is no more then what is false and vain,
And merely mortal dross;
So little is our loss,
So little is thy gain.
For when as each thing bad thou hast entombed,
And last of all, thy greedy self consumed,
Then long Eternity shall greet our bliss
With an individual kiss,
And Joy shall overtake us as a flood;
When every thing that is sincerely good
And perfectly divine,
With Truth, and Peace and Love shall ever shine
About the supreme Throne
Of him to whose happy-making sight alone,
When once our heavenly-guided soul shall climb;
Then all this earthly grossness quit,
Attired with stars, we shall for ever sit,
Triumphing over Death, and Chance, and thee
      O Time.

Notes on selected words. *Leaden-stepping*: slowly moving. *Plummet*: the weight on a clock that keeps the mechanism ticking. *Mortal*: fleeting and ending in death. *Dross*: leftover and worthless particles or residue. *Individual*: in addition to its usual meaning, undivided and therefore eternal or everlasting. *Perfectly*: in addition to its usual meaning, completely. *Grossness*: corruption; imperfection. *Quit*: left behind permanently.

Commentary. The fleetingness of earthly life and the swift passing of time have been a preoccupation of poets throughout history. The label that the human race has bestowed on human mutability and the transience of life is "the problem of time." Milton's poem "On Time" deals with the problem of time and asserts a Christian consolation in the face of that problem. The occasion of the poem is suggested by a canceled manuscript title—"to be set on a clock-case." The poem thus has the character of an inscription intended for an impressive clock operated with weights (what today we call a "grandfather clock").

The poem is a taunt addressed from start to finish to a personified Time, and it invites comparison with John Donne's famous taunt to a personified Death ("Death, be not proud," see page 72). The poem divides thematically into two parts, each consisting of a single long sentence (the second one being *very* long). Lines 1–8 are a rude put-down of Time as merely destroying what is perishable and unimportant. Lines 9–22 celebrate what Christians will enjoy in heaven in eternity. In this section we are led to meditate on the joys of heaven, as the poem awakens our longing for the eternal world.

The simple design of the poem is rendered pleasingly complex by numerous individual touches that invite exploration. Milton uses an intermixture of three conventional rhyme schemes—*abab* (quatrain), *aa* (couplet), and *abba* (enclosed rhyme). The poetic texture is comprised of numerous individual images and comparisons, but in addition there are several image patterns—eating, running/walking, the process of refining away impurities, light, and the heavenly or transcendent. The negative connotations of the images in the first eight lines are played off against the positive associations of the second part of the poem dealing with eternity. An evocative biblical allusion climaxes the poem: the picture of believers being "attired with stars" is a reference to Daniel 12:3, which pictures the resurrected righteous as shining "like the stars forever and ever."

How Soon Hath Time

JOHN MILTON (1608–1674)

How soon hath Time, the subtle thief of youth,
Stolen on his wing my three and twentieth year!
My hasting days fly on with full career,
But my late spring no bud or blossom showeth.
Perhaps my semblance might deceive the truth
That I to manhood am arrived so near,
And inward ripeness doth much less appear,
That some more timely-happy spirits endueth.
Yet be it less or more, or soon or slow,
It shall be still in strictest measure even
To that same lot, however mean or high,
Toward which Time leads me, and the will of Heaven.
All is, if I have grace to use it so,
As ever in my great Task-Master's eye.

Notes on selected words. *Subtle*: working imperceptibly and deviously. *Hasting*: hastening. *Career*: speed. *Semblance*: outer appearance. *Endueth*: endows. *Lot*: destiny. *Mean*: modest; humble; lowly. *Heaven*: metonymy for God. *All is*: all that matters is. *It* (line 13): time. *Ever*: always.

Commentary. This is an occasional poem (a poem arising from a specific occasion in the life and times of the poet) written around the time of

Milton's twenty-third birthday. Milton used that occasion to take stock of his situation as he was nearing the end of his college education at Cambridge University. What he found (and expresses in the poem) was a sense of underachievement and immaturity, with which he comes to grips in an awareness of the swift passing of time. At least that is what the octave of this Italian sonnet presents—a version of senior panic.

However, the word *yet* at the beginning of line 9 is the reversal that is conventional in the Italian sonnet. Whereas the octave poses the problem of underachievement heightened by the problem of time's passing, the sestet is a statement of consolation based on two favorite Puritan doctrines—divine providence and the intertwined concepts of calling/vocation and stewardship. There is also a passing reference to the classical idea of time leading a person to his or her determined destiny.

The poem is Milton's meditation on his situation, but literature is universal as well as particularized, so we should apply the poet's thinking about the problems of time and underachievement to ourselves. As we overhear Milton's self-accusation in the octave, we might well hear the notes of our own sense of failing to achieve what we or others have expected of us, and also our troubling awareness that we are mutable and that time keeps passing. The octave is an anxiety vision, and it is beneficial to confront our anxieties instead of denying them. The frame of reference in the octave is human rather than religious.

The sestet, however, expresses an explicitly Christian consolation within which we can remain calm and confident even in the face of the problems of time and underachievement. The first Christian note is submission to divine providence, whatever it might bring to a person. The phrase *the will of Heaven* is code language (technically a metonymy) for "the will and providence of God." Whatever God has determined for the speaker's life (and ours), that is sufficient for anyone who possesses faith in God's goodness. Then when the concluding two lines speak of God as *the great Task-Master*, the Reformation and Puritan doctrine of stewardship springs into view. God is the one who calls people to their tasks in the world, and a person is answerable to God, not human expectations of success. Faithfulness in service to God, and living in conscious awareness of his oversight and approval, are what matter.

Of course all of this is embodied in a poem dense with poetic texture, biblical allusions, and grand syntax (sentence structure). These are things that deserve our close analysis; in fact, the devotional effect of the poem depends on our taking the time for such analysis.

Lady That in the Prime of Earliest Youth

JOHN MILTON (1608–1674)

Lady that in the prime of earliest youth
Wisely has shunned the broad way and the green,
And with those few art eminently seen
That labor up the hill of heavenly Truth,
The better part with Mary and with Ruth
Chosen thou hast; and they that overween
And at thy growing virtues fret their spleen,
No anger find in thee, but pity and ruth.
Thy care is fixed and zealously attends
To fill thy odorous lamp with deeds of light,
And hope that reaps not shame. Therefore be sure
Thou, when the Bridegroom with his feastful friends
Passes to bliss at the mid-hour of night,
Hast gained thy entrance, virgin wise and pure.

——— ∞ ———

Notes on selected words. *Eminently*: to a notable degree. *Overween*: are arrogant and overbearing. *Ruth*: pity, but the word is also a pun on Ruth, the Old Testament heroine, so that the associations become "having the character qualities of Ruth." *Odorous*: fragrant. *Feastful*: festive; joyful.

Commentary. This is another occasional sonnet by Milton, but we need to infer the occasion from the poem itself. We have here a poetic version of a note of encouragement to a fellow Christian. We can picture Milton in the role of mature adult encouraging an adolescent or young teenager who had taken him into her confidence regarding criticism that she had received (perhaps from an unbelieving family) for the earnestness of her commitment to Christ. As a confidant of the girl (perhaps a family friend), Milton commends her for having chosen "the better part" (like Mary the friend of Jesus who sat at his feet; see Luke 10:42) and encourages her to persevere in the Christian life. We need to remind ourselves that although literature is filled with particulars, it is also a mirror in which we see universal human experience, including our own. This poem holds up a model of Christian commitment that we ourselves should aspire to emulate.

The subject of the poem is Christian virtue, or living a serious Christian life. The theme (interpretive slant) is that cultivating the Christian virtues as the young woman of the sonnet does prepares a person for heaven. This "note of spiritual encouragement" thus asserts that the goal of life is to cultivate the spiritual virtues as a preparation for heaven. The poem is structured on a temporal contrast between present endeavor and future reward, and other contrasts then cluster under that—the broad way versus the narrow way, worldly lifestyle versus godly lifestyle, foolishness versus wisdom, lack of preparedness versus preparedness.

The poem is a mosaic of biblical allusions. The four major biblical passages from which Milton constructed his poem are the following: Jesus's contrast in the Sermon on the Mount between the broad way that leads to destruction and the narrow way that leads to life (Matt. 7:13–14); the story of Mary and Martha (Luke 10:38–42); the love story of Ruth and Boaz (Ruth 1–4); and the parable of the wise and foolish virgins, with its emphasis on preparedness versus lack of preparedness (Matt. 25:1–13). Famous archetypes also figure prominently—the hill of virtue, the hill of difficulty, the path or way (divided into a wide path leading to destruction and a narrow path leading to life), the woman of virtue, and the wise woman.

When Faith and Love

JOHN MILTON (1608–1674)

When Faith and Love, which parted from thee never,
Had ripened thy just soul to dwell with God,
Meekly thou didst resign this earthy load
Of death, called life, which us from life doth sever.
Thy works and alms and all thy good endeavor
Stayed not behind, nor in the grave were trod,
But as Faith pointed with her golden rod,
Followed thee up to joy and bliss for ever.
Love led them on, and Faith, who knew them best,
Thy hand-maids, clad them o're with purple beams
And azure wings, that up they flew so dressed,
And spake the truth of thee on glorious themes
Before the Judge, who thenceforth bid thee rest
And drink thy fill of pure immortal streams.

Notes on selected words. *Sever*: divide. *Trod*: stepped on. *Hand-maids*: female servants. *Clad*: clothed. *O'er*: over. *Azure*: sky-blue. *Spake*: spoke.

Commentary. This sonnet is an occasional poem, as signaled by the title that was affixed to the poem when it was published: "On the religious memory of Mrs. Catharine Thomason, my Christian friend, deceased December 1646." As we read the poem, we might well picture

Milton standing at the gravesite of his departed friend. The central motif around which the poem is constructed is a journey of transition from earth to heaven. Various image patterns cluster around that motif—moving from one place to another, leave-taking, transferring, guiding, arriving at a destination, possessions coming behind, donning new clothes, being welcomed upon arrival, settling into a new abode, resting after a journey, and a celebratory drink upon arrival.

The poem follows the conventional pattern of Puritan funeral sermons for women. A feature of such sermons is that they are based on a single verse from the Bible. Milton's sonnet takes Revelation 14:13 for its text; in Milton's King James Version, the text reads, "Blessed are the dead which die in the Lord from henceforth: Yea, saith the Spirit, that they may rest from their labours; and their works do follow them." Milton ranges beyond this single text, but this verse provides the basic plotline. Another standard feature of funeral sermons for women was a eulogy for the deceased that painted a portrait of godliness to be emulated by the listeners.

The poem has a narrative flow and a single progressive action that are difficult to divide into separate phases. With a little streamlining, we can divide the poem as follows: lines 1–4 announce the death of Mrs. Thomason in the brief statement that she resigned her earthly life; lines 5–13a tell the story of how the deeds of the deceased also made the journey from earth to heaven and commended the deeds of Mrs. Thomason to God the Judge; in lines 13b–14, she receives her reward of immortal rest.

The content of the poem draws heavily upon an important theological issue that was prominent in Milton's day. The concepts of faith and love (meaning works springing from love) were at the heart of the debate between Protestants and Catholics between grace and merit. Milton's poem shows its Puritan allegiance by making faith the basis of salvation and works the result and proof of faith.

Avenge, O Lord, Thy Slaughtered Saints

JOHN MILTON (1608–1674)

Avenge, O Lord, thy slaughtered saints, whose bones
Lie scattered on the Alpine mountains cold,
Even them who kept thy truth so pure of old,
When all our fathers worshiped stocks and stones;
Forget not: in thy book record their groans,
Who were thy sheep, and in their ancient fold
Slain by the bloody Piedmontese, that rolled
Mother with infant down the rocks. Their moans
The vales redoubled to the hills, and they
To heaven. Their martyred blood and ashes sow
O'er all the Italian fields, where still doth sway
The triple Tyrant; that from these may grow
A hundredfold, who, having learned thy way,
Early may fly the Babylonian woe.

Notes on selected words. *Worshiped stocks and stones*: an allusion to Jeremiah 3:9, which pictures the idolatrous Israelites as worshiping "with stone and tree"; Milton intends this image of idolatry as a picture of Roman Catholicism, and he is critical of his native England for embracing the Reformation later than European nations, especially the early-day Waldensians of the poem. *Fold*: a sheepfold, but also any enclosed piece of ground; Milton is painting a picture of the Alpine valleys where the Waldensians had lived for several centuries. *Bloody*: bloody-minded and also blood-smeared. *Redoubled*: echoed back. *The triple Tyrant*: the Catholic Pope. *Fly*: escape from; turn away from; repudiate. *Babylonian*: Roman Catholic; an allusion to the fall of Babylon in Revelation 18. *Woe*: the woe caused by the Catholic Church, and also the woe or judgment coming upon it, along the lines of "flee[ing] from the wrath to come" (Luke 3:7).

Commentary. The occasion of this poem was the "Piedmontese Easter" of April 24, 1655, when Roman Catholic soldiers from Italy massacred 1,712 men, women, and children of the Waldensians living in the Alpine mountains and valleys. The Waldensians were very early Protestants who already in 1215 were driven out of Italy and forced to settle in the Alps. Milton's poem recreates some of the atrocities that occurred.

As a devotional poem, this Italian sonnet prompts us to think about what is a godly response to terrible violence against God's followers. The poet's response to the atrocity is thoroughly rooted in the Bible. Two Bible verses are particularly relevant. One is Romans 12:19: "Vengeance is mine, I will repay, says the Lord." In the first eleven and a half lines, the poet prays to God to avenge the slaughter of the Waldesians. The gruesome details in the poem are not in the mode of the imprecatory Psalms, where the speaker asks that God inflict physical calamity on his enemies, but are instead a picture of the violence that has already occurred and that demands justice. Starting in the middle of line 11, the poem modulates from a prayer for punishment to a prayer for redemption, as the poet pictures the Italian Catholics repenting of their sins of violence and learning to follow God's true way. Second Peter 3:9 can be viewed as a subtext here, which pictures God as "not wishing that any should perish, but that all should reach repentance."

The poem's form is as rooted in the Bible as the content is. The genre on which the poem is modeled is the psalm of lament; elements that Milton imported from that genre are an introductory cry to God to act; a vivid portrait of the injustice that requires a response; petition to God to do specific things; and a reversal of mood in which the poet states his confidence in God (which here takes the form of a prayer for the redemption of the murderers). The language of Milton's sonnet is so thoroughly biblical that all but five words appear in the King James Version. All these biblical elements contribute to the tone of religious indignation for which the poem is famous.

When I Consider How My Light Is Spent

JOHN MILTON (1608–1674)

When I consider how my light is spent,
Ere half my days in this dark world and wide,
And that one talent which is death to hide
Lodged with me useless, though my soul more bent
To serve therewith my Maker, and present
My true account, lest he returning chide;
"Doth God exact day-labor, light denied?"
I fondly ask. But Patience, to prevent
That murmur, soon replies, "God doth not need
Either man's work or his own gifts; who best
Bear his mild yoke, they serve him best. His state
Is kingly. Thousands at his bidding speed
And post o'er land and ocean without rest:
They also serve who only stand and wait."

———— ∞∞∞ ————

Notes on selected words. *Ere*: before. *Bent*: desirous. *Chide*: scold.
Doth: does. *Exact*: require. *Day-labor*: work performed by laborers
who are hired by the day, as in Jesus's parable of the workers in the
vineyard (Matt. 20:1–16). *Fondly*: foolishly. *Thousands*: thousands of
angels. *His*: God's. *Post*: travel. *O'er*: over.

Commentary. The occasion of this sonnet is Milton's becoming totally blind at the age of forty-four. An early editor coined what became the familiar title for the poem—"On His Blindness." The poem develops two lines of thought, both encapsulated in the last line (*They also serve who only stand and wait*). On the one hand, the poem is a statement of resignation, as the poet expresses an implied submission to the situation of standing and waiting. But the poem is also a statement of justification, as the poet finds a way to assert that *they also serve* who *only stand and wait*. The poet's meditation is based on an underlying quest motif in which he searches for and finds a way to serve God acceptably. The poem is built around the implied question, What does it take to please God? The entire poem assumes that God requires service, and the key verb *serve* appears three times.

This poem is constructed on the classic two-part structure of the Italian sonnet. The argument in the first seven and a half lines is that God requires active service in the world. This line of thought becomes an increasingly intense anxiety vision for the blind poet, who cannot perform active service. The sestet then offers an alternative type of service, placed into the mouth of a personified Patience. The alternate service consists of standing and waiting, and this has multiple meanings. It is an image of monarchy, first of all, and is offered as a picture of serving God in heaven as the angels do, in praise and worship. The last line also evokes a picture of a life of private retirement, out of the public eye, and it is helpful at this point to know that before Milton became blind he was a famous international figure in his role as international secretary to Oliver Cromwell.

The poem is a mosaic of biblical allusions. Particularly prominent are the parable of the workers in the vineyard (Matt. 20:1–16) and the parable of the talents (Matt. 25:14–30). Both parables portray God as the master who calls workers to their tasks and as the judge who rewards stewards for active service and punishes them for sloth. Also important is Jesus's famous saying about doing the works of his Father "while it is day; night is coming, when no one can work" (John 9:4). The last three lines are based on angelology (the study of angels), and the contrast between active angels who fly about the world and contemplative angels who remain in God's heavenly court.

Methought I Saw My Late Espoused Saint

JOHN MILTON (1608–1674)

Methought I saw my late espoused saint,
Brought to me like Alcestis from the grave,
Whom Jove's great son to her glad husband gave,
Rescued from death by force though pale and faint.
Mine, as whom washed from spot of childbed taint
Purification in the old law did save,
And such as yet once more I trust to have
Full sight of her in heaven without restraint,
Came vested all in white, pure as her mind.
Her face was veiled, yet to my fancied sight
Love, sweetness, goodness, in her person shined
So clear, as in no face with more delight.
But O, as to embrace me she inclined,
I waked, she fled, and day brought back my night.

───∞───

Notes on selected words. *Late*: recently deceased. *Espoused*: married; the "late espoused saint" is thus Milton's deceased wife. *Mine*: my wife; there is an ellipsis after the word *wife*, so in our mind we reach forward to the verb *came* four lines down, inserting it in our mind after *mine* (mine *came*). *As whom*: another ellipsis, as we supply the word

131

one before *whom* (as *one* whom). *Old law*: Old Testament, or perhaps specifically the Mosaic law regarding the purification laws for mothers after childbirth (Lev. 12:1–8). *Vested*: dressed. *Fancied*: existing in the poet's imagination or dream.

Commentary. The occasion of this love sonnet is the death of Milton's second wife (Katherine Woodcock Milton), who died in childbirth, as the age called it (technically, two months after giving birth to a daughter, who also died). The poem records a real or imagined dream of the glorified Katherine in heaven and Milton's longing to be reunited with her. The poem has a narrative structure in which we relive the sequence that made up the vision of the glorified woman. Line 1 introduces the narrative situation of the poet's dream; lines 2–12 record the content of the dream; and lines 13–14 return to the narrative frame and tell how the vision vanished.

Within the three-part story noted above, the central part of the poem—the portrait of the deceased wife—unfolds in four phases. First Milton's wife is compared to a famous wife from classical mythology, Alcestis, who gave her life as a ransom for her husband and then was restored to her husband through the intervention of Hercules. Then Milton compares his wife to Old Testament mothers who were saved by performing the purification laws for women after delivering a baby. Third, Milton describes his wife in terms of a hoped-for reunion in heaven. Finally, Milton describes his wife in terms of her spiritual qualities as a glorified saint in heaven.

We cannot remind ourselves too often that even though literature is filled with particulars, those particulars are a net that captures the universal—not just one person's experience but many people's experiences. This poem gives shape to such universal experiences as grief, longing for a deceased spouse and loved one, love longing, redemption, sanctification, and glorification in heaven. Enhancing this universality are certain powerful archetypes (universal images and motifs that recur throughout literature and life): the *donna angelicata* (the angelical woman, deceased, glorified in heaven, and wearing white); longing for a deceased beloved; the sorrowing survivor; imagery that distances the otherworldly, in this case dream and veil; reunion of beloveds; and white as a symbol of purity.

Greatly Instructed
I Shall Hence Depart

JOHN MILTON (1608–1674)

Greatly instructed I shall hence depart,
Greatly in peace of thought, and have my fill
Of knowledge, what this vessel can contain,
Beyond which was my folly to aspire.
Henceforth I learn that to obey is best,
And love with fear the only God, to walk
As in his presence, ever to observe
His providence, and on him sole depend,
Merciful over all his works, with good
Still overcoming evil, and by small
Accomplishing great things, by things deemed weak
Subverting worldly-strong, and worldly-wise
By simply meek; that suffering for Truth's sake
Is fortitude to highest victory,
And to the faithful death the gate of life—
Taught this by his example whom I now
Acknowledge my Redeemer ever blest.

———◦◦◦———

Notes on selected words. *Hence*: from here. *This vessel*: my mind; alternatively, I as a person. *Deemed*: considered. *Subverting*: undermining the power of. *Worldly-strong*: strong by worldly standards.

Worldly-wise: wise by worldly standards. *Fortitude*: strength and courage in the face of adversity.

Commentary. These lines come near the end of Milton's epic poem *Paradise Lost*. They are spoken by the human protagonist of the story, Adam, and they are the moment of epiphany (supreme insight) toward which the whole poem moves. The epic story has covered the whole span of history from creation through the fall and its aftermath through redemption in Christ and to the final consummation of history. Adam's words represent his final insight after receiving a vision of future history (fallen but redeemed through the atoning death of Christ) from the angel Michael, whom God dispatched from heaven to instruct Adam and Eve about how to endure life in a fallen world (a veritable survival kit).

Adam's speech can be read devotionally as a summary of the Christian life. It specifically encapsulates the knowledge that will enable a believer to live life as God intends it in a fallen world. The poem expresses the key that unlocks a meaningful life. Each line or pair of lines adds something important to the total picture. These lines are a statement of the knowledge that matters most for any person. In the context of the Western epic tradition, this passage is the culmination of Milton's revamping of the value structure of the martial (military) epic. While retaining the military language of the epic with such words as *overcoming, accomplishing great things, fortitude*, and *highest victory*, Milton spiritualizes the inherited motifs. This passage is Milton's new epic standard of what is good, and it climaxes in coming to trust in Christ as Savior (last line).

Rendering even more devotional energy to the passage is a network of Bible passages that underlie the poem as a subtext. One of these is 1 Corinthians 1:18–31, with its put-down of worldly strength and wisdom and its elevation of spiritual values. The statement that "to obey is best" is rooted in a continuous theme of the Bible, where the vocabulary of *obey, obedience*, and *keeping God's commandments* appears 250 times. The picture of God as *merciful over all his works* echoes Psalm 145:9 ("his mercy is over all that he has made"), and the statement *with good still overcoming evil* echoes Romans 12:21 ("overcome evil with good"). The rousing statement that *to the faithful* death is *the gate of life* alludes to Revelation 2:10 ("Be faithful unto death, and I will give you the crown of life"). And so forth.

Verses upon the Burning of Our House, July 10th, 1666

ANNE BRADSTREET (1612–1672)

In silent night when rest I took,
For sorrow near I did not look,
I wakened was with thundering noise
And piteous shrieks of dreadful voice.
That fearful sound of "fire" and "fire"
Let no man know is my desire.
I starting up, the light did spy,
And to my God my heart did cry
To straighten me in my distress
And not to leave me succorless.
Then coming out, behold a space
The flame consume my dwelling place.
And when I could no longer look,
I blessed his grace that gave and took,
That laid my goods now in the dust.
Yea, so it was, and so 'twas just.
It was his own; it was not mine.
Far be it that I should repine,
He might of all justly bereft
But yet sufficient for us left.
When by the ruins oft I passed
My sorrowing eyes aside did cast
And here and there the places spy
Where oft I sat and long did lie.
Here stood that trunk, and there that chest,

There lay that store I counted best;
My pleasant things in ashes lie
And them behold no more shall I.
Under the roof no guest shall sit,
Nor at thy table eat a bit.
No pleasant talk shall 'ere be told
Nor things recounted done of old.
No candle 'ere shall shine in thee,
Nor bridegroom's voice 'ere heard
    shall be.
In silence ever shalt thou lie.
Adieu, adieu, all's vanity.
Then straight I 'gin my heart to chide:
And did thy wealth on earth abide,
Didst fix thy hope on moldering dust,
The arm of flesh didst make thy trust?
Raise up thy thoughts above the sky
That dunghill mists away may fly.
Thou hast a house on high erect,
Framed by that mighty Architect,
With glory richly furnished
Stands permanent, though this be fled.
It's purchased and paid for too
By him who hath enough to do.
A price so vast as is unknown,
Yet by his gift is made thine own.
There's wealth enough; I need no more.
Farewell, my pelf; farewell, my store.
The world no longer let me love;
My hope and treasure lies above.

Notes on selected words. *Let no man know is my desire*: I hope that no person will know the fearful sound of "fire, fire." *Spy*: catch sight of. *Straighten me*: strengthen me; alternatively, set me upright or on a straight path. *Succorless*: without help in time of distress. *Repine*: complain. *Bereft*: deprived of. *Thee*: my former house. *Adieu*: farewell. *Vanity*: emptiness. *'Gin*: begin. *Chide*: scold. *Moldering*: decaying. *Framed*: built. *Hath enough to do*: has done enough, a reference to the sufficiency of Christ's work of redemption. *Pelf*: money or riches. *Store*: abundance.

Commentary. The complete title of this poem upon its first publication was as follows: "Here follow some verses upon the burning of our house, July 10, 1666." The poem obviously belongs to the genre of occasional poem, meaning that it arose from a specific occasion in the poet's life. The occasion is recreated in the opening lines of the poem, namely, the house fire that destroyed the Bradstreet home. This poem raises the same question as the poem of a fellow Puritan, John Milton's sonnet on his blindness: What consolation is adequate when we lose something that would seem to be indispensable to earthly life?

The first twelve lines recreate the disaster of the fire. This is the point of departure for the poet's meditation in which she comes to grips with her loss. The unstated quest of the poet during the course of her meditation is to find adequate repose in the face of her feelings of loss occasioned by the fire. The quest does not follow a straight line but instead moves back and forth between the two motifs of lamenting the loss and finding acceptance in the primacy of the spiritual. The pitfall that a poet needs to avoid in a poem like this is allowing the consolation to come across as facile (too easily achieved and glibly stated). Bradstreet meets the challenge by fully acknowledging the human and earthly loss that she has sustained.

Several sub-points cluster under the two main motifs of lament and resignation. The poem follows the flow of the poet's thought process in a manner that today we call "stream of consciousness." Under the theme of lament, the poet (a) describes her ruined possessions lying in the ashes, and (b) lists common household events that will never again occur in the house. Under the theme of resignation, the poet (a) asserts that God, not she, was the owner of the house, (b) rebukes herself for putting her affection on earthly possessions and securities, and (c) takes consolation in knowing that God and heaven are her ultimate wealth. The poem is written in simple eight-syllable couplets, befitting the simple piety that it expresses.

It is a truism that a reader's response to a work of literature is self-revealing. Non-Christian literary critics regularly claim that the sense of loss is stronger in this poem than the consolation. Christian readers who share Anne Bradstreet's scale of values experience the poem as the poet intended.

Poverty

THOMAS TRAHERNE (1636–1674)

As in the house I sat,
Alone and desolate,
No creature but the fire and I,
The chimney and the stool, I lift mine eye
Up to the wall,
And in the silent hall,
Saw nothing mine
But some few cups and dishes shine,
The table and the wooden stools
Where people used to dine;
A painted cloth there was,
Wherein some ancient story wrought,
A little entertained my thought,
Which light discovered through the glass.

I wondered much to see
That all my wealth should be
Confined in such a little room,
Yet hope for more I scarcely durst presume.
It grieved me sore
That such a scanty store
Should be my all;
For I forgot my ease and health,
Nor did I think of hands or eyes,
Nor soul nor body prize;
I neither thought the sun,
Nor moon, nor stars, nor people mine,

Though they did round about me shine;
And therefore was I quite undone.

Some greater things, I thought,
Must needs for me be wrought,
Which till my craving mind could see
I ever should lament my poverty;
I fain would have
Whatever bounty gave,
Nor could there be
Without or love or deity;
For should not he be infinite
Whose hand created me?
Ten thousand absent things
Did vex my poor and wanting mind,
Which, till I be no longer blind,
Let me not see the King of kings.

His love must surely be
Rich, infinite, and free;
Nor can he be thought a God
Of grace and power, that fills not his abode,
His holy court,
In kind and liberal sort;
Joys and pleasures,
Plenty of jewels, goods, and treasures,
To enrich the poor, cheer the forlorn,
His palace must adorn,
And given all to me;
For till his works my wealth became,
No love or peace did me inflame:
But now I have a Deity.

***

Notes on selected words. *But*: except. *Painted cloth*: table cloth with a painted picture imprinted on it. *Ancient story*: familiar story from long ago, perhaps taken from the Bible. *Wrought* (line 12): was artistically formed. *Entertained my thought*: captured my thought; held my attention. *Discovered*: revealed. *Durst*: dared. *Scanty store*: meager supply of goods. *Was . . . undone*: felt ruined or destroyed; or alternatively, felt incomplete [as in "not done"]. *Must needs*: must necessarily. *Wrought* (line 30): done or accomplished. *Fain*: gladly. *Nor could there be*: we need to supply the word *bounty* at the end of the line. *Or love*: either love. *Vex*: trouble. *Wanting mind*: mind preoccupied with supposed lacks. *Abode*: dwelling or house.

Commentary. This narrative poem is a statement of personal testimony on the theme of 1 Timothy 6:6—"godliness with contentment is great gain." The poem embodies that truth in a simple narrative of personal discovery as the speaker sits in his home. Each stanza contributes a phase to this story of discovery. In the opening stanza, the poet "composes the scene" by situating himself in the solitary setting of his meager kitchen. In the second stanza he subjects this scene to analysis and laments the poverty of his situation. In the next stanza the speaker comes to his senses and chastises himself for not rising above the material realm of physical possessions. The final stanza is the poem's moment of epiphany (revelation and insight), as the speaker takes stock of the riches he possesses in God.

The poem is an example of how the simple can become an object of beauty and profundity. The very simplicity of the story that the poet tells us lends universality to the action, so that we can walk into the poem and make the experience our own. Additionally, as we ponder the action that unfolds, we can discern certain powerful paradoxes of the Christian life. Less is more, especially when the speaker's lack of physical possessions leads him to lay claim to God (the ultimate *more*). Losing is gaining, as the speaker's lack of physical plenty leads him to gain God. Poverty in the realm of physical possessions becomes riches if it leads one to embrace God as the ultimate wealth. These paradoxes all lead to the climactic last line in which the poet declares where his quest has ended.

As we continue to ponder the poem, a grand contrast of imagery gradually takes shape in our awareness. On one side we have images of minimalism—*chimney, stool, a few cups and dishes, wooden stools*. On the other side we find vast images of *moon, stars, bounty, jewels, treasures*, and *palace*. The speaker moves from one world to another as his spiritual insight increases.

Peace

HENRY VAUGHAN (1621–1695)

My soul, there is a country
Afar beyond the stars,
Where stands a wingéd sentry
All skillful in the wars;
There above noise and danger
Sweet Peace sits crowned with smiles,
And One born in a manger
Commands the beauteous files.
He is thy gracious friend,
And (O my soul awake!)
Did in pure love descend
To die here for thy sake.
If thou canst get but thither,
There grows the flower of peace,
The rose that cannot wither,
Thy fortress, and thy ease.
Leave then thy foolish ranges;
For none can thee secure,
But One who never changes,
Thy God, thy life, thy cure.

Notes on selected words. *Afar*: a great distance away. *Wingéd sentry*: a sentry is an armed guard or watchman; the designation "wingéd sentry" is implied to be plural and refers to the angelic host of heaven. *One*: Christ. *Beauteous*: beautiful. *Files*: rows of the angelic host. *Canst*: can. *Thither*: there. *Ease*: freedom from pain or distress. *Ranges*: wandering. *Secure*: make permanently safe.

Commentary. The genre of this poem is well known in devotional poetry, namely, the poet's address to his own soul. Psalm 103, for example, begins, "Bless the LORD, O my soul." Often such self-addresses are phrased in the format of a command (as this poem does four lines from the end), but even when they are not, the implied situation is that of an exhortation, as the soul is admonished and encouraged to "set itself in right tune" (as Milton termed it)—a kind of spiritual safety inspection. Sometimes the soul is commanded to correct its current state, as in the refrain of Psalms 42 and 43: "Why are you cast down, O my soul?" Vaughan's poem, written in the simple quatrain verse form (*abab*), does all these things.

The subject of this poem is heaven, and as the poem turns that prism in the light, we are led to contemplate various dimensions of heaven. The unifying focus is heaven as a place (*a country*) of peace and security that transcends earthly agitation and insecurity. The poem can be divided into four movements. First the poem situates us in the safe place of heaven (lines 1–6); contemplative traditions speak of "composing the scene." Then the poet shifts our contemplation from the place to the person and work of Christ (lines 7–12), whose sacrifice makes possible the believer's entry into heaven. Next the poem returns to a description of heaven (lines 13–16), with emphasis on its immortal freedom from earthly strife. In the last four lines, the soul is scolded for attempting to find security in something other than heaven, accompanied by a reminder that only God can be the ultimate safety of the soul.

The winsome surface simplicity of the poem becomes more complex as we look closely at the verbal artifact that Vaughan has created. The poem presents images that tap our deepest longings for permanence and total satisfaction, and we need to luxuriate over each of these evocative images. Paradox (apparent contraction or striking contrast that needs to be unraveled) also lends complexity to the poem. For example, the poem celebrates heaven as a place of peace and freedom from strife, yet there is a thread of military imagery in the poem. The opening image of heaven as *a country* seems to promise that the poem will emphasize heaven as a place, yet half of the poem is about the person of Christ. The poem foregrounds the serenity of heaven, yet the speaker's address to his soul sounds an implied warning that the soul can lose heaven if it does not rouse itself to action.

Easter Hymn

HENRY VAUGHAN (1621–1695)

Death and darkness, get you packing,
Nothing now to man is lacking,
All your triumphs now are ended,
And what Adam marred is mended.
Graves are beds now for the weary,
Death a nap, to wake more merry;
Youth now, full of pious duty,
Seeks in thee for perfect beauty;
The weak and aged tired with length
Of days, from thee look for new strength;
And infants with thy pangs contest
As pleasant, as if with the breast.
Then, unto him who thus hath thrown
Even to contempt thy kingdom down,
And by his blood did us advance
Unto his own inheritance,
To him be glory, power, praise,
From this, unto the last of days.

Notes on selected words. *Get you packing*: go away; be on your way. *What Adam marred*: what Adam destroyed by the fall. *Merry*: happy. *Youth*: young people as a group. *Pangs*: pains. *Contest*: enter into conflict with. *The breast*: their mother's breast.

Commentary. The apostle Paul gave the prototype of a confident taunt addressed to a personified death on the basis of Christ's resurrection from the dead. Here is that prototype: "O death, where is your victory? O death, where is your sting?" (1 Cor. 15:55). This passage gave John Donne the impetus for his famous address to death that begins, "Death, be not proud" (see page 72). Knowing what we do about Henry Vaughan's imitation of specific poems by his predecessor George Herbert, it is entirely possible that his "Easter Hymn" is indebted to Donne's famous sonnet.

Whereas Donne addresses death in a formal rhetorical manner, as though it were occurring in a courtroom, Vaughan's approach is much more colloquial, as though he were pushing an unwelcome intruder off his front porch: *Death and darkness, get you packing* (the equivalent, perhaps, of "scram"). If Donne's poem takes our breath away with its audacious put-down of death, it nonetheless seems somewhat timid compared to the energy with which Vaughan harangues death. The contempt with which Vaughan treats death, and the extremity of his claims that people desire death, can best be interpreted as rooted in the technique of hyperbole (conscious exaggeration for the sake of emotional effect). A poem like this is not literally true, but it expresses what it *feels* like to believe in immortality based on the resurrection at the last day.

We can note the following things about the artistic form of the poem. It is written in simple couplets and four-foot (eight-syllable) lines. The first four lines announce the main idea or thesis of the poem. The next eight lines support the opening generalization with specific examples of how through various categories people can embrace death as something positive and desirable. Of course those assertions are based on a belief that death is (as Milton called it in *Paradise Lost*) "the gate of life." The last six lines are a benediction collated from benedictions in the epistles (Eph. 3:20–21; Heb.13:20–21; Jude 24–25; Rev. 1:5–6).

The Dawning

HENRY VAUGHAN (1621–1695)

Ah! What time wilt Thou come? When
    shall that cry,
"The bridegroom's coming" fill the sky?
Shall it in the evening run,
When our words and works are done?
Or will Thy all-surprising light
Break at midnight,
When either sleep or some dark pleasure
Possesseth mad man without measure?
Or shall these early fragrant hours
Unlock Thy bowers,
And with their blush of light descry
Thy locks crowned with eternity?
Indeed, it is the only time
That with Thy glory doth best chime;
Full hymns doth yield,
The whole creation shakes off night,
And for Thy shadow looks the light;
Stars now vanish without number,
The pursy clouds disband and scatter,
All expect some sudden matter;
Not one beam triumphs, but from far
That morning star.
Oh, at what time soever, Thou,
Unknown to us, the heavens wilt bow,
And with Thy angels in the van
Descend to judge poor careless man,

Grant I may not like puddle lie
In a corrupt security,
Where, if a traveler water crave,
He finds it dead and in a grave.
But as this restless vocal spring
All day and night doth run and sing,
And though here born, yet is acquainted
Elsewhere, and flowing keeps untainted,
So let me all my busy age
In Thy free services engage.
And though while here of force I must
Have commerce sometimes with poor dust,
And in my flesh, though vile and low,
As this doth in her channel flow,
Yet let my course, my aim, my love,
And chief acquaintance be above.
So when that day and hour shall come
In which Thyself will be the sun,
Thou will find me dressed and on
     my way,
Watching the break of Thy great Day.

Notes on selected words. *Wilt*: will. *Run*: occur. *Some dark pleasure*: some forbidden act. *Mad man*: irrational person, living life apart from Christ. *These early fragrant hours*: sunrise; early morning. *Descry*: disclose; reveal. *Locks*: locks of hair. *Chime*: harmonize with; agree with. *Doth yield*: occur. *Pursy*: literally fat and short-winded; here meaning clouds that are large and disappearing. *Matter*: momentous event. *Triumphs*: shines. *But*: except. *At what time soever*: at whatever time. *Thou . . . the heavens wilt bow*: you will descend from heaven. *In the van*: in the forefront. *Dead and in a grave*: vanished; alternatively, stagnant and undrinkable (an extension of the puddle image three lines earlier). *Restless vocal spring*: gurgling and noisy spring of water. *Here born*: has its origin. *Is acquainted Elsewhere*: flows in a stream to places far removed from its point of origin. *Age*: life. *Here*: on earth; during my earthly life. *Have commerce sometimes with poor dust*: sometimes busy myself with merely earthly matters. *Vile and low*: corrupt and low on a scale of merit. *Course*: stream of water, metaphoric of a person's life. *Thy great Day*: the day of Christ's second coming; the last day.

Commentary. This poem is a meditation on the second coming of Jesus. The overall effect of the poem is to impress upon us the need to be ready for the return of Christ. The poem can be viewed as a meditation on Luke 12:37–38: "Blessed are those servants whom the master finds awake when he comes. . . . If he comes in the second watch, or in the third, and finds them awake, blessed are those servants!" Taking his cue from the motif of alternate times for the return of Jesus (the second watch or the third), Vaughan begins his poem with a catalog of possible times of the day when Jesus might return. The purpose is not to engage in idle speculation but rather to lead us to picture the return as a way of making it palpable to us. Making experience vivid is what the imagination does best.

The list of alternate times for the return ends with morning, which is declared most appropriate for the return of Christ. The title of the poem comes into view here, as the dawn assumes a symbolic force of a new day and new age. The second half of the poem is an extended prayer ("colloquy," in the parlance of meditative tradition) in which the speaker asks that he will be found watchful rather than sidetracked by earthly preoccupations when Jesus returns.

Vaughan belongs to the metaphysical school of seventeenth-century poetry, a tradition that is known as being "metaphorically strong," by which is meant an inclination to embody the meanings of a poem in striking metaphors and analogies. Vaughan elaborates two metaphors at such length that they can be said to embody the primary meaning of the poem. One is the image of the dawn of a new day, first introduced in the title and returning with climactic force in the last line of the poem. The second metaphor involves a stream that flows far from its point of origin. Vaughan uses this image to picture the way in which in our daily course of activities we naturally find ourselves engaged in earthly pursuits, and yet our goal lies beyond these in our eternal home. The poem is about priorities, and in the prayer that comes to dominate it, the speaker asks to be spared from being diverted from lesser matters and instead be awake when the great day of Christ's return dawns.

The Waterfall

HENRY VAUGHAN (1621–1695)

With what deep murmurs through time's silent
    stealth
Doth thy transparent, cool, and watery wealth
  Here flowing fall,
  And chide, and call,
As if his liquid, loose retinue stayed
Lingering, and were of this steep place afraid,
  The common pass
  Where, clear as glass,
  All must descend
  Not to an end,
But quickened by this deep and rocky grave,
Rise to a longer course more bright and brave.

Dear stream! Dear bank, where often I
Have sate and pleased my pensive eye,
Why, since each drop of thy quick store
Runs thither whence it flowed before,
Should poor souls fear a shade or night,
Who came, sure, from a sea of light?
Or since those drops are all sent back
So sure to thee, that none doth lack,
Why should frail flesh doubt any more
That what God takes, he'll not restore?

O useful element and clear!
My sacred wash and cleanser here,

My first consigner unto those
Fountains of life where the Lamb goes!
What sublime truths and wholesome themes
Lodge in thy mystical deep streams!
Such as dull man can never find
Unless that Spirit lead his mind
Which first upon thy face did move,
And hatched all with his quickening love.
As this loud brook's incessant fall
In streaming rings restagnates all,
Which reach by course the bank, and then
Are no more seen, just so pass men.
O my invisible estate,
My glorious liberty, still late!
Thou art the channel my soul seeks,
Not this with cataracts and creeks.

Notes on selected words. *Through time's silent stealth*: unobtrusively or unnoticed over a long period of time; the image of time as a thief is archetypal. *Chide*: scold (in reference to the roaring of the water at the bottom of the waterfall). *Retinue*: official traveling group. *The common pass*: the path over which all must pass. *Quickened*: enlivened; accelerated; made more active. *Rise to a longer course*: come up to the surface after the depths of the plunge and then continue to flow in a stream. *Brave*: excellent (archaic). *Pensive*: thoughtful; contemplative. *Element*: aspect of nature. *Consigner*: agent who hands over; in three lines here Vaughan merges the waters of baptism and an allusion to Revelation 7:17, with its picture of Christ as the Lamb who guides his followers to springs of living water. *That Spirit*: the Holy Spirit. *Which first upon thy face did move*: the reference in this line and the next is to Genesis 1:2, with its account of how the Spirit of God moved upon the face of the waters when God created the world. *Quickening*: life-giving. *In streaming rings*: in concentric rings moving outward in ripples from the center point where the water lands at the bottom of the waterfall. *Restagnates*: makes calm again. *My invisible estate*: my home in heaven. *Still late*: still delayed and waiting to happen.

Commentary. This is first of all a nature poem that should be relished as such. Henry Vaughan was a nature lover who frequented sites near his Welsh home in the valley of the River Usk, including the waterfall about which he wrote in this poem. Considered as a nature poem, "The Waterfall" would be right at home alongside nature poetry by nineteenth-century Romantic poet William Wordsworth. But Vaughan belonged to the seventeenth-century school of poets known as the metaphysical poets, whose ranks included John Donne and George Herbert. For Christian poets like these, nature is more (but not less) than a physical phenomenon. It is also a signpost to spiritual reality.

The poem belongs to the genre of the meditative landscape poem. The first item of business to be transacted in such a poem is to situate the poet in a landscape. This is what occurs in the opening stanza, which does a marvelous job of recreating the sensations of the stream as it pools at the top of the waterfall and then plunges down, only to continue its course. In the extended middle of the poem (ending five lines from the end), the poet addresses the stream by means of the poetic technique known as "apostrophe"—an address to something absent and/or inanimate as though it were capable of hearing. This extended address to the stream gives us variations on a single theme: just as the stream continues beyond the waterfall to an invisible destination, so Christians upon death do not cease to live but continue their life in heaven.

Thus far the poem has followed the expected pattern prescribed by a traditional meditative tradition, beginning with the "composition of the scene" and then moving to analysis of the opening situation. In the last four lines, Vaughan moves to the conventional prayer or colloquy. In it, he addresses his *invisible estate*—heavenly home—and affirms that this is his true and ultimate channel or passageway to *glorious liberty*.

The artistry of the poem is magnificent. The division into stanzas can easily obscure that the poem is written in simple couplets. The poem is a triumph of nature description. Symbolism abounds. So do evocative biblical allusions, which in the third stanza include Revelation 7:17; 1 Corinthians 2:9–11; Genesis 1:2; and Romans 8:21.

They Are All Gone into the World of Light

HENRY VAUGHAN (1621–1695)

They are all gone into the world of light!
And I alone sit lingering here;
Their very memory is fair and bright,
And my sad thoughts doth clear.

It glows and glitters in my cloudy breast,
Like stars upon some gloomy grove,
Or those faint beams in which this hill is dressed,
After the sun's remove.

I see them walking in an air of glory,
Whose light doth trample on my days:
My days, which are at best but dull and hoary,
Mere glimmering and decays.

O holy Hope and high Humility,
High as the heavens above,
These are your walks, and you have showed them me
To kindle my cold love.

Dear, beauteous Death, the jewel of the just,
Shining nowhere but in the dark,
What mysteries do lie beyond thy dust,
Could man outlook that mark!

He that hath found some fledged bird's nest may know
At first sight if the bird be flown;

But what fair well or grove he sings in now,
That is to him unknown.

And yet as angels in some brighter dreams
Call to the soul, when man doth sleep,
So some strange thoughts transcend our wonted themes
And into glory peep.

If a star were confined into a tomb,
Her captive flames must needs burn there;
But when the hand that locked her up gives room,
She'll shine through all the sphere.

O Father of eternal life, and all
Created glories under thee,
Resume thy spirit from this world of thrall
Into true liberty.

Either disperse these mists, which blot and fill
My perspective still as they pass,
Or else remove me hence unto that hill,
Where I shall need no glass.

———⚬⚬⚬———

Notes on selected words. *It* (line 5): heaven, the world of light. *Hoary*: gray. *Beauteous*: beautiful. *Outlook thy mark*: see over that boundary. *Fledged bird*: young bird able to fly. *Well*: spring of water. *Wonted themes*: accustomed thoughts. *Gives room*: releases the star from an enclosed tomb or enclosure. *All the sphere*: the whole world. *Resume thy spirit*: take your creature (presumably the speaker in the poem) back to yourself. *Thrall*: slavery or bondage. *My perspective*: my telescope; by extension, my vision of distant things. *Still*: always. *That hill*: heaven. *Glass*: telescope.

Commentary. The subject of this poem is longing for heaven. We infer from the opening stanzas that it is an occasional poem that had its origin in the poet's contemplation of his deceased friends and family members. Additionally, Vaughan made a practice of climbing a famous Welsh hill behind his house and viewing the night sky through a telescope, so it is easy to imagine such an occasion for the contemplation that he records in this poem.

Before we explore Vaughan's highly original treatment of his theme, we can profitably note conventional Christian motifs that enter the poem. The apostle Paul claimed that to depart this life for heaven "is far better" than remaining on earth, declaring this to be his "desire" (Phil. 1:23). Late in *Paradise Lost*, Milton calls death "the gate of life" for those who believe in Christ (see page 133). Additionally, the biblical world view is based on the premise of two worlds—an unseen heavenly and spiritual world (the transcendent "other world") and the visible earthly world. Our experience of the spiritual world is indistinct and leaves us longing to see it more completely; the apostle Paul compared it to seeing "in a mirror dimly" (1 Cor. 13:12). All of these motifs feed into Vaughan's poem, which portrays the transcendent realm of heaven as being qualitatively better than our earthly sphere.

In the first three stanzas, the poet describes his imagined vision of departed loved ones living in heaven. Images of stars and light evoke a picture of the transcendent other world. Having "composed the scene" (as devotional manuals term it), in the next four stanzas the poet analyzes the implications of the vision of heaven that he has recounted. The general thrust of the meditation is to lend sanction to thinking about heaven and longing for it. The last two stanzas are the expected prayer or colloquy in which the speaker asks God to grant a clearer vision of heaven or remove him from earth to heaven.

C. S. Lewis, in his chapter on hope in *Mere Christianity*, offers his opinion that "a continual looking forward to the eternal world is . . . one of the things a Christian is meant to do." Poems about heaven such as this one by Vaughan enable us do it.

When in Mid-Air, the Golden Trump Shall Sound

JOHN DRYDEN (1631–1700)

When in mid-air, the golden trump shall sound,
To raise the nations under ground;
When in the valley of Jehosophat,
The Judging God shall close the book of fate,
And there the last Assizes keep,
For those who wake, and those who sleep;
When rattling bones together fly,
From the four corners of the sky;
When sinews o'er the skeletons are spread,
Those clothed with flesh, and life inspires the dead;
The sacred poets first shall hear the sound,
And foremost from the tomb shall bound:
For they are covered with the lightest ground,
And straight, with in-born vigor, on the wing,
Like mounting larks, to the new morning sing.
There thou, sweet saint, before the choir shall go,
As harbinger of Heav'n, the way to show,
The way which thou so well hast learned below.

Notes on selected words. *Mid-air*: the sky. *Golden trump*: the trumpet that will sound the advent of the last day and final judgment. *Valley of Jehosophat*: the place of the last judgment (see Joel 3:2, 12). *Last Assizes*: final court of judgment. *Those who wake*: those who are still alive when the day of judgment arrives. *Those who sleep*: those who are dead. *Thou, sweet saint*: Anne Killigrew, subject of the poem. *Harbinger*: forerunner; someone sent ahead to announce what will follow. *Below*: on earth; during your earthly life.

Commentary. This is the last stanza of a ten-stanza ode that is familiarly known in English literature as "Ode on the Death of Mrs. Ann Killigrew." John Dryden wrote the poem in honor of an artistic and musical friend when she died of smallpox at the age of twenty-five. The first nine stanzas of the poem are a panegyric that praises the virtues and artistic abilities of Anne Killigrew in the mode of polite compliment. These stanzas belong to the realm of the literature of clarification and common experience, not of explicit Christian belief. They are edifying in a humanistic way as affirming worthy human values and artistic talent.

In the final stanza, printed here as a freestanding poem, the frame of reference becomes specifically Christian, as Dryden imagines the last day and final judgment in all their glory. It is one of the finest monuments of the apocalyptic or eschatological imagination. A common technique in devotional literature is known as "composing the scene," meaning that the person meditating or composing a poem begins by imagining himself or herself present at an event mentioned in the Bible. In this exalted poem, Dryden imagines the last day and final judgment (in a manner that invites comparison with a sonnet by John Donne that begins "At the round earth's imagined corners, blow your trumpets, angels," see page 69).

Dryden secures his effect with an exalted style, especially a suspended sentence in which a series of parallel subordinate *when* clauses makes us keep reading for nine whole lines before we reach the main clause of the sentence, beginning, *The sacred poets first shall hear the sound*. The second half of the passage is a bit of fantasy in which Dryden pictures poets as rising first at the final resurrection, but even here the soaring apocalyptic imagination lifts us up with its pictures of bodies bounding from the grave and ascending larks and the rise of a new morning.

The devotional splendor of the passage consists of the energy with which we experience resurrection day in our imaginations. Our daily routine lulls us into thinking that earthly life is all that exists. An exalted rendition of the last day of Christian eschatology lifts us above this illusion.

Veni, Creator Spiritus
["Come, Creator Spirit"]

JOHN DRYDEN (1631–1700)

Creator Spirit, by whose aid
The world's foundations first were laid,
Come, visit every pious mind;
Come, pour thy joys on human kind;
From sin and sorrow set us free,
And make thy temples worthy Thee.
　　O, source of uncreated Light,
The Father's promised Paraclete!
Thrice Holy Fount, thrice Holy Fire,
Our hearts with heavenly love inspire;
Come, and thy sacred unction bring
To sanctify us, while we sing!
　　Plenteous of grace, descend from high,
Rich in thy seven-fold energy!
Thou strength of his almighty hand,
Whose power does heaven and earth
　　　　command,
Proceeding Spirit, our defense,
Who dost the gift of tongues dispense,
And crowns thy gift with eloquence!
　　Refine and purge our earthly parts;
But, oh, inflame and fire our hearts!
Our frailties help, our vice control;
Submit the senses to the soul;
And when rebellious they are grown,

Then lay thy hand and hold them down.
    Chase from our minds the Infernal Foe;
And peace, the fruit of love, bestow;
And, lest our feet should step astray,
Protect and guide us in the way.
    Make us eternal truths receive,
And practice all that we believe:
Give us thyself, that we may see
The Father and the Son, by thee.
    Immortal honor, endless fame,
Attend the Almighty Father's name:
The Savior Son be glorified,
Who for lost man's redemption died:
And equal adoration be,
Eternal Paraclete, to thee.

Notes on selected words. *Thy temples*: your people, or those who believe in you, on the strength of 1 Corinthians 6:19, which declares that Christians' bodies are temples of the Holy Spirit. *Paraclete*: New Testament word for the Holy Spirit, meaning one who comes alongside and/or one who serves as an advocate and/or one who intercedes. *Unction*: anointing. *Earthly parts*: bodies and minds. *The Infernal Foe*: Satan.

Commentary. Earlier in this anthology, George Herbert's adaptation of Psalm 23 (see page 98) was offered as a representative of a voluminous tradition in English and American poetry known as the metrical psalms. With this poem by neoclassical poet John Dryden we come to a parallel phenomenon—an English poem based on an ancient non-biblical text. *Veni, Creator Spiritus* was a medieval Latin hymn. Being a hymn, it was composed in four-line stanzas. Literal translations of this Latin hymn preserve this stanzaic arrangement, packaged in short four-foot (eight syllable) lines.

    Even a cursory look at the format of Dryden's poem shows that he has composed an English poem that asks to be experienced as an original poem. It borrows certain materials from the Latin original but makes no attempt to reproduce it. Dryden's poem was originally printed as a single continuous poem instead of separated stanzas. The indented units (not separate stanzas) are variable in length, ranging from four lines to seven lines. Further unity is imposed by the verse form in which Dryden composed his poem, namely, couplets (virtually the required verse form in the neoclassical "age of reason"). Freed from a preoccupation with whether Dryden translated the medieval hymn correctly, we can relish the poem in its own right.

This poem is one of the most exalted religious lyrics in the English language. We can note first that the poem is a continuous prayer addressed to the Holy Spirit. The language and sentiments are exalted, expressed in what literary scholars call the high style. An exuberance breathes through the words and sentiments. Furthermore, the poem is a virtual compendium (succinct collection) of all the important biblical passages on the Holy Spirit. It is nothing less than a primer—a collection of first principles—on the doctrine of the Holy Sprit. Taking time to match lines in the poem to biblical passages will provide a substantial devotional experience, both instructive and edifying.

The Spacious Firmament on High

JOSEPH ADDISON (1672–1719)

The spacious firmament on high,
With all the blue ethereal sky
And spangled heavens, a shining frame
Their great Original proclaim.
The unwearied sun, from day to day,
Does his creator's powers display,
And publishes to every land
The work of an almighty hand.

Soon as the evening shades prevail
The moon takes up the wondrous tale,
And nightly to the listening earth
Repeats the story of her birth;
While all the stars that round her burn
And all the planets in their turn,
Confirm the tidings as they roll,
And spread the truth from pole to pole.

What though in solemn silence all
Move round the dark terrestrial ball?
What though no real voice nor sound
Amid the radiant orbs be found?
In reason's ear they all rejoice,
And utter forth a glorious voice,
Forever singing as they shine,
"The hand that made us is divine."

Notes on selected words. *Firmament*: sky. *Ethereal*: heavenly. *Spangled*: sparkling. *Frame*: in this context, form; artifact; thing made. *Their great Original*: their divine Creator, God. *Burn*: shine. *Tidings*: news. *Terrestrial ball*: earthly sphere or planet. *Orbs*: orbits. *Reason's*: the mind's.

Commentary. Although this poem eventually became a familiar Christian hymn, it was composed by a literary person or "man of letters" and published as a poem in a famous eighteenth-century literary magazine called *The Spectator*. When it was first published, the poem was preceded by an explanatory headnote from which we learn four important things that can aid us as we assimilate the poem: (1) Addison wrote the poem as part of his defense of the idea that the creation is an argument for the existence of God; (2) the poem is modeled on Psalm 19, which similarly views the heavenly bodies as a revelation designed to teach us about God; (3) Addison called his poem an ode (an exalted poem on a grand theme written in the high style); (4) the poem illustrates what the eighteenth century called "the sublime" (the large and awe-inspiring parts of creation, in implied contrast to "the picturesque"). All four of these features are embodied in the poem and are an avenue to an initial analysis of it.

Although the poem is an ode, it is also modeled on the biblical psalm of praise. As such, it praises God and the wonder of the heavenly bodies. Like the nature psalms, this poem simultaneously praises nature and the God of nature.

Addison's poem is what literary scholars today call an "intertextual" work that depends for its effect on an implied interaction with a previous text. The pre-text for Addison's poem is Psalm 19:1–4. Virtually every line in Addison's poem either repeats or elaborates upon something in Psalm 19:1–4. For example, Psalm 19 takes the daily circuits of the sun and moon as its subject, and it treats both of these natural phenomena as revealing the glory of God. Furthermore, the psalmist does a lot with the paradox of the "silent message" of the heavenly bodies: the sun and moon metaphorically express a message and can therefore be credited with conveying "speech," but because there is no *literal or audible* speech, the poem paradoxically asserts that "there is no [audible] speech" (Ps. 19:3). Addison's poem is an elaboration of all these motifs from Psalm 19, without which the poem would not exist. As a devotional poem, this poem is doxological, moving us to praise God.

When Rising from
the Bed of Death

JOSEPH ADDISON (1672–1719)

When, rising from the bed of death,
O'erwhelmed with guilt and fear,
I see my Maker face to face,
O how shall I appear?

If yet, while pardon may be found,
And mercy may be sought,
My heart with inward horror shrinks,
And trembles at the thought.

When thou, O Lord, shalt stand disclosed
In majesty severe,
And sit in judgment on my soul,
O how shall I appear?

But thou hast told the troubled mind
Who does her sins lament,
The timely tribute of her tears
Shall endless woes prevent.

Then see the sorrow of my heart,
Ere yet it be too late,
And hear my Savior's dying groans,
To give these sorrows weight.

For never shall my soul despair
Her pardon to procure,

Who knows thine only Son has died
To make her pardon sure.

⸻ ❦ ⸻

Notes on selected words. *Bed of death*: deathbed; the poet begins by picturing the moment immediately after death. *How shall I appear*: what will be my spiritual standing; how can I stand acquitted before God's judgment seat? *Timely*: occurring in time. *Tribute*: payment made to meet an obligation; an offering that proves the reality of one's attitude (e.g., tears as a tribute or testimony to one's contrition). *These sorrows*: the speaker's sorrows. *Weight*: efficacy. *Procure*: obtain.

Commentary. This poem was composed by Addison during an illness and was first published in the famous literary magazine of the time called *The Spectator*. The poem is built around the implied situation of a dying person's imagining what it will be like to face God as judge immediately after physical death. In the background lies a biblical verse such as Hebrews 9:27—"It is appointed for man to die once, and after that comes judgment." The speaker begins his contemplation in a stance of terror at divine judgment, and on this point the poem is reminiscent of several similar poems of dying terror authored by John Donne. From this initial problem, the poem unfolds as a quest to find peace of mind and soul. Written in simple quatrains rhyming *abcb*, the poem expresses an equally simple piety based on the essence of the gospel (forgiveness of sin through the sacrifice of Christ).

The poem is based on a central contrast between the first three stanzas and the concluding three stanzas. The first three stanzas express the speaker's fear of final judgment. The experience placed before us is rooted in familiar Christian doctrine and experience, expressed in conventional Christian vocabulary. Thus the sinful soul is burdened with *guilt* and the sinner with *fear*. To this day we speak of *facing one's Maker* upon death. The transcendent God *sits in judgment* on the individual soul. *Pardon and mercy* are what we need to *seek*. In three simple stanzas, Addison makes the essential human predicament vivid to us.

165

The final three stanzas express the consolation of the gospel in equally bedrock terms. Sorrow for sin (the theme of the contrite heart) is expressed with the vocabulary of *sins lamented, tears,* and *sorrows of the heart.* The atoning death of Jesus comes alive with the picture of the *Savior's dying groans* and God's *only Son [who] has died.* The sinner's *troubled mind* and *soul's despair* find a solution in God's *pardon sure.* There is nothing fancy in the poem but only the basics. The poem is nothing less that a primer on the Christian doctrines of sin and salvation, encapsulated in the meditations of a dying penitent.

The Dying Christian to His Soul

ALEXANDER POPE (1688–1744)

Vital spark of heavenly flame!
Quit, O quit, this mortal frame;
Trembling, hoping, lingering, flying,
O the pain, the bliss of dying!
Cease, fond Nature, cease thy strife,
And let me languish into life.

Hark! They whisper; angels say,
Sister Spirit, come away!
What is this absorbs me quite?
Steals my senses, shuts my sight,
Drowns my spirits, draws my breath?
Tell me, my soul, can this be death?

The world recedes; it disappears!
Heaven opens on my eyes! My ears
With sounds seraphic ring!
Lend, lend your wings! I mount! I fly!
O Grave! Where is thy victory?
O Death! Where is thy sting?

Notes on selected words. *Vital spark of heavenly flame*: the soul. *Quit*: leave. *Mortal frame*: human body. *Fond*: foolish. *Languish*: gradually waste away and then depart. *Absorbs me quite*: totally occupies my attention. *Seraphic*: angelic.

Commentary. This poem is built around the premise stated in the title, as the poet imagines his own moment of death and departure for heaven. The speaker pictures himself on his deathbed and addresses his own soul. This imagined experience is portrayed in such a way as to make the poem a statement of belief in the immortality of the Christian's soul, a familiar theme in Christian devotional poetry.

The author of this poem belongs to the neoclassic era, or "age of reason," so it is surprising that the poem is such a highly emotional and affective lyric, filled with exclamations and apostrophes (addresses to absent or personified phenomena as though they are present and can hear). The poem presents the experience of departing this life as a kaleidoscope of sensations and fleeting thoughts, as the poem flits from one subject to another in a frenzy of excitement. No living person has undergone and recorded the actual experience of leaving this life for the next, but many poets have imagined what it will be like, as Pope does in this poem. The Bible enjoins us to be watchful and prepared for death when it comes, and a devotional poem like this can help us down that path.

Although the poem possesses the ever-shifting flux noted above, certain constants throughout the poem enable us to experience it as a unity. The key to finding this unity is an awareness of a two-tier or two-sphere universe consisting of a series of dichotomies. These include soul and body, heaven and earth, temporary life in this world and eternal life in heaven. As the poem traverses back and forth among these contrasts, we quickly sense a unifying tone or mood, namely, the speaker's joy to be leaving earthly life for heavenly life. We sense a total lack of sorrow over the end of earthly life. The speaker is impatient to be moving on. The climax comes in the two concluding lines, which Pope alludes to from 1 Corinthians 15:55.

This song is a song of hope in the face of death, but it is not everyone's song. As the title asserts, it is the song of a Christian's soul. Only the believing soul can view death as a moment of victory and triumph rather than defeat and despair.

Huswifery

EDWARD TAYLOR (1642–1729)

Make me, O Lord, Thy spinning-wheel complete.
Thy holy word my distaff make for me.
Make mine affections Thy swift flyers neat,
And make my soul Thy holy spool to be.
My conversation make to be Thy reel,
And reel thy yarn thereon spun of Thy wheel.

Make me Thy loom then, knit therein this twine,
And make Thy Holy Spirit, Lord, wind quills:
Then weave the web Thyself. Thy yarn is fine.
Thine ordinances make my fulling-mills.
Then dye the same in heavenly colors choice,
All pinked with varnished flowers of paradise.

Then clothe therewith mine understanding, will,
Affections, judgment, conscience, memory,
My words and actions, that their shine may fill
My ways with glory and Thee glorify.
Then mine apparel shall display before Ye
That I am clothed in holy robes for glory.

—————◎✕✕◎—————

Notes on selected words. *Huswifery*: housekeeping; the actions per-
formed by a housewife. *Distaff, flyers, spool, reel, loom, knit, twine,
quills, web, fulling-mills, dye*: these words all name specific parts of a

spinning wheel or the process of weaving cloth. *Affections*: emotions and desires. *Ordinances*: commands; rules for living. *Pinked*: decorated. *Varnished*: shiny.

Commentary. All of the poets included in this anthology are distinctive as individuals, illustrating the evocative description in 1 Peter 4:10 of being "good stewards of God's varied grace." A few of them are so distinctive and idiosyncratic as to warrant the designation of being unique—one of a kind. The Puritan New England poet Edward Taylor is one of these, and his poem "Huswifery" is something of a shock to anyone for whom this is the first encounter with Taylor.

Taylor is an American manifestation of the metaphysical school of seventeenth-century poetry. John Donne and George Herbert belong to the same group, whose poetry is above all metaphorically strong, meaning that the message of their poems resides especially in their striking comparisons. Poets always rely on metaphor and simile to some extent, but usually the analogies are either conventional or plausible. The metaphysical poets reached for original comparisons, and often ingenious or farfetched ones. Edward Taylor takes that impulse to its farthest extreme. Metaphysical poets also sometimes built entire poems around a single controlling metaphor. Taylor does all of these things in his most famous poem.

"Huswifery" (the work of a housewife) is built around the controlling metaphor of creating a garment and then being clothed in it. We do not need to know the technical meanings of all the words related to that central image, but we need to have the overall action in view: the speaker wishes to be clothed in the glory of God. In elaborating this central action, the poet describes three separate phases of garment making, corresponding to the three stanzas of the poem: spinning the wool into yarn or thread, weaving the thread into cloth, and putting the finished garment on a person. In the final stanza Taylor lists the human faculties that he wishes to be clothed in God's garment, and when the inventory is complete, we can see that the poem is a prayer to God for sanctification (becoming like God). The last line clinches the point: *That I am clothed in holy robes for glory.*

Infinity, When All Things It Beheld

EDWARD TAYLOR (1642–1729)

Infinity, when all things it beheld
In nothing, and of nothing all did build,
Upon what base was fixed the lathe wherein
He turned this globe, and rigalled it so trim?
Who blew the bellows of his furnace vast?
Or held the mold wherein the world was cast?
Who laid its corner stone? Or whose command?
Where stand the pillars upon which it stands?
Who laced and filleted the earth so fine,
With rivers like green ribbons smaragdine?
Who made the seas its selvedge, and it locks
Like a quilt ball within a silver box?
Who spread its canopy? Or curtains spun?
Who in this bowling alley bowled the sun?
Who made it always when it rises set:
To go at once both down, and up to get?
Who the curtain rods made for this tapestry?
Who hung the twinkling lanterns in the sky?
Who? Who did this? or who is he? Why, know
It's only Might Almighty this did do.
His hand hath made this noble work which stands
His glorious handiwork not made by hands,
Who spoke all things from nothing, and with ease.

Notes on selected words. *Lathe*: rotating horizontal wheel or disk used in shaping wood, metal, pottery, etc. *This globe*: the round earth. *Rigalled it*: not known for certain; suggestions include giving it finishing touches, or making it in the shape of a circle or ring, or making it grooved. *Trim*: neat. *Filleted*: bound; alternatively, furnished or adorned. *Smaragdine*: green like emerald. *Selvedge*: edge or border (a term from sewing, where it means the edge of woven cloth). *Quilt ball*: ball whose cover is made from sewn pieces of cloth.

Commentary. The selection printed here is half of a poem that Taylor composed as "The Preface" to a long poem entitled *God's Determinations Touching His Elect*. The excerpt is a self-contained creation poem that celebrates God's handiwork in creating the world. The basic technique comes straight from several famous creation poems in the Old Testament and consists of a list of questions regarding God's acts of creation. For example, in the voice from the whirlwind in Job 38–41, God asks eighty scientific questions along the lines of, "Who shut in the sea with doors . . . [and] made clouds its garment?" (38:8–9). Isaiah 40:12–26 is cut from the same cloth, with questions such as "Who has measured the waters in the hollow of his hand?" (v. 12).

Taylor takes this motif of the catalog of questions and makes it his own. Like the biblical poets noted above, Taylor chose everyday images to show how easily God can control the vast forces of nature. Taylor's "metaphysical" style controls what he does, a style that specialized in ingenious comparisons. Thus the earth itself is like a globe fashioned on a potter's lathe, the sun is a bowling ball, and adorning the earth is like sewing a garment. We are intended to analyze each analogy and marvel at the poet's ingenuity in composing it, as well as the aptness of the image for the natural phenomenon that is described. The overall effect is to domesticate wonder—to make the power and mystery of nature seem like part of the everyday routine.

When Christian poets write nature poems, they make them doxological (starting with the five nature psalms in the book of Psalms). They first awaken our admiration for nature, and then they deflect the praise for it to God the Creator. This is the genius of Taylor's poem.

The Resignation

Thomas Chatterton (1752–1770)

O God, whose thunder shakes the sky,
Whose eye this atom globe surveys,
To thee, my only rock, I fly,
Thy mercy in thy justice praise.

The mystic mazes of thy will,
The shadows of celestial light,
Are past the power of human skill,
But what the Eternal acts is right.

O teach me in the trying hour,
When anguish swells the dewy tear,
To still my sorrows, own thy power,
Thy goodness love, thy justice fear.

If in this bosom aught but Thee
Encroaching sought a boundless sway,
Omniscience could the danger see,
And Mercy look the cause away.

Then why, my soul, dost thou complain?
Why drooping seek the dark recess?
Shake off the melancholy chain,
For God created all to bless.

But ah! My breast is human still;
The rising sigh, the falling tear,
My languid vitals' feeble rill,
The sickness of my soul declare.

But yet, with fortitude resigned,
I'll thank the inflictor of the blow;
Forbid the sigh, compose my mind,
Nor let the gush of misery flow.

The gloomy mantle of the night,
Which on my sinking spirit steals,
Will vanish at the morning light,
Which God, my East, my sun reveals.

———⊗⊗⊗———

Notes on selected words. *Atom globe*: either round globe or tiny globe. *Mystic*: mysterious; supernaturally devised. *Mazes*: complex network of pathways. *The Eternal*: God. *Swells the dewy tear*: brings tears to the eyes. *Own*: claim as my own. *Aught*: anything. *Sought a boundless sway*: attempted a complete control of me. *Omniscience*: the omniscient or all-knowing God. *Look the cause away*: see to it that the cause was removed. *The dark recess*: the place of despair. *Vitals*: vital signs that the body is functioning. *Rill*: small stream. *The inflictor*: the one who inflicts.

Commentary. The literary family to which this poem belongs is named in the title: it is a poem of resignation. Other notable members of that family in this anthology include Milton's sonnet on his blindness and Tennyson's poem "Crossing the Bar" (see pages 129 and 198). The worldly mind thinks that resignation is weakness, but the believing mind knows that submission to God is strength.

The strategy in a poem of resignation is to combine three sets of data. The starting premise is a condition of dissonance and disequilibrium—a situation that causes the speaker to be troubled and agitated. In Chatterton's poem, we find this side of the equation in a continuous thread of references to *shadows, night, trying hour, sorrows, danger, gush of misery*, and many more in this vein, from the thunder of the opening line to the gloomy mantle of the night four lines from the end. Dissonance is part of the logic of a poem of resignation: if there were no troubling situation, resignation would be unnecessary.

The second ingredient is the state of contentment and equilibrium that the speaker finds in spite of the troubling situation. Instead of fighting against the opposition, the speaker submits to it and finds peace of mind. In Milton's sonnet on his blindness, the poet divides the poem into two halves: first the problem, then the solution and resignation. By contrast, Chatterton mingles the two, setting up a process of vacillation between trouble and consolation. The effect is to capture the struggle that we often experience in real life between resistance and resignation.

Third, there needs to be a sufficient basis for resigning oneself to a hostile situation. In poems of resignation written by Christians, God and his providence are that sufficient reason. Chatterton's poem does a marvelous job of keeping the focus on God, right from the opening phrase. In fact, the first half of the poem is a prayer addressed to God, making the resignation personal. Resignation like this is a choice, and the second half of the poem accordingly consists of "self talk," in the mode of the speaker's address to his own soul in Psalms 42 and 43 ("Why are you cast down, O my soul?"). In Chatterton's poem this self-address begins with the line, *Then why, my soul . . . ?*

The Lamb

WILLIAM BLAKE (1757–1827)

Little Lamb who made thee?
Dost thou know who made thee?
Gave thee life and bid thee feed,
By the stream and o'er the mead;
Gave thee clothing of delight,
Softest clothing wooly bright;
Gave thee such a tender voice,
Making all the vales rejoice!
Little Lamb who made thee?
Dost thou know who made thee?

Little Lamb, I'll tell thee,
Little Lamb, I'll tell thee!
He is callèd by thy name,
For he calls himself a Lamb:
He is meek and he is mild,
He became a little child:
I a child and thou a lamb,
We are callèd by his name.
Little Lamb, God bless thee.
Little Lamb, God bless thee.

Notes on selected words. *Mead*: meadow. *Vales*: valleys.

Commentary. The key to relishing this poem is to be receptive of its childlike qualities. For starters, it was published in a volume of Blake's poems entitled *Songs of Innocence and Experience* in which the poet divided human experience into a child's perspective and an adult's perspective. This poem embodies a child's experience of nature and life. Additionally, "The Lamb" may have been influenced by a child's hymn authored by Charles Wesley and first printed three decades before Blake's poem in *Hymns and Sacred Poems*; the hymn begins with the line, "Gentle Jesus, meek and mild" (with two of those words appearing in line 15 of Blake's poem), and there are other carryovers as well, including lines that read "thou wast once a little child" and "Christ, the holy child, in me."

Though written for adult readers of Blake's volume, this poem nonetheless expresses life as a child perceives it. The verse form is simple couplets, arranged invitingly into two ten-line stanzas. The question and answer format is childlike. In fact, we can say that Blake gives the lamb a catechism lesson based on the first question and answer in the *Westminster Catechism for Young Children*: "Who made you?" "God." The technique of consecutively repeated lines conveys the effect of a nursery rhyme as well as lending a songlike quality to the poem. The adjectives and descriptive details ascribed to the lamb evoke a child's view of the world. The speaker identifies himself as a child four lines from the end.

Turning to the religious content of the poem, it is no exaggeration to say that the speaker gives the lamb a theology lesson in two brief stanzas. The first stanza celebrates God's creation of the world, and the second stanza explains Christ's redemption as the sacrificial lamb of God. The incarnation is present in the assertion that Christ "became a little child." Our imaginations reach out as well to other biblical passages that draw upon the archetype of the lamb, and a famous gospel narrative (Mark 10:13–16) where Jesus welcomes children and blesses them, as Blake also does in the last two lines.

And Did Those Feet

WILLIAM BLAKE (1757–1827)

And did those feet in ancient time,
Walk upon England's mountains green?
And was the holy Lamb of God
On England's pleasant pastures seen?

And did the Countenance Divine,
Shine forth upon our clouded hills?
And was Jerusalem builded here,
Among these dark Satanic mills?

Bring me my bow of burning gold;
Bring me my arrows of desire;
Bring me my spear: O clouds unfold!
Bring me my chariot of fire!

I will not cease from mental fight,
Nor shall my sword sleep in my hand,
Till we have built Jerusalem
In England's green and pleasant Land.

Notes on selected words. *Those feet*: the feet of Jesus. *Countenance Divine*: face of God, an allusion to the Aaronic benediction, which includes the prayer that "the LORD lift up his countenance upon you"

(Num. 6:26). *Clouded hills*: not a negative image of industrial pollution but a reference to an endearing feature of the island nation of England, namely, the puffy white clouds that are a frequent feature of the sky. *Jerusalem*: a new society founded on biblical and Christian principles. *Dark Satanic mills*: the factories that accompanied the industrial revolution. *Bring me my bow* . . . : metaphors for non-military resistance to the trends of the time; the images come from various prophetic and apocalyptic passages in the Bible (e.g., Isa. 66:15 and Jer. 4:13).

Commentary. This poem has the status of a folk hymn in England, and a look at sources on the Internet shows that the poem is pervasive in English society and culture. It has been set to music many times. In view of this massive cultural and multi-media presence, we need to remind ourselves that this text began as an ordinary poem, printed as part of a preface to a long poem by William Blake.

This poem is a prophetic poem in the mode of Old Testament prophetic books. Old Testament prophetic books devote the most space to (1) a description and denunciation of the moral corruption of society in the prophet's day, and (2) a command to end the degeneration and establish a new society founded in righteousness. These two elements also make up Blake's poem, which literary scholars place into the genre of social protest.

The social context of Blake's protest is the industrial revolution of the nineteenth century. A single evocative phrase is all that Blake needs to establish what has occasioned the poem: *dark Satanic mills*. This is "code language" for industrial factories and cities that are polluted both physically and morally.

The other context about which we need to know is the medieval Glastonbury legend. Glastonbury Tor [a hill] is a very tall hill in the middle of England with green fields around it. The hill was once an island surrounded by swampland reaching to the sea. It was the Avalon of the Arthurian legend. According to the collective medieval imagination, Jesus accompanied his uncle Joseph of Arimethea to this island at the age of twelve, and then he returned to the island before starting his public ministry, building a wattle hut that became the first Christian church in England. He also prepared for his mission of establishing a new age, which Blake simply calls Jerusalem (based on the imagery of Revelation). This myth has no basis in fact, but Blake uses it in the first two stanzas to evoke a picture of England's Christian past to which society must return if it is to have any hope of being a good society. The first two stanzas are a series of incredulous questions that express amazement, in light of what civilization has become, that England could actually have once been a Christian society. Because Blake uses the Glastonbury legend as the basis of the first two stanzas, the Christian past to which the poem calls the present age to return focuses specifically on the person of Jesus.

The military imagery of the last two stanzas is Blake's call to return to the Christian past and its values (as pictured in the first two stanzas). Christians today surely see things the same way, and the poem says what they too want to say, only it says it more eloquently. Blake does not envision a military battle but a battle in which the weapons are the pen and words—a battle for people's minds and souls. Blake's military metaphors of bows and arrows and such like come from apocalyptic passages in the Bible such as Isaiah 66:15–16 and Jeremiah 4:13.

The Destruction of Sennacherib

LORD BYRON (GEORGE GORDON BYRON)

(1788–1824)

The Assyrian came down like the wolf on the fold,
And his cohorts were gleaming in purple and gold;
And the sheen of their spears was like stars on the sea,
When the blue wave rolls nightly on deep Galilee.

Like the leaves of the forest when summer is green,
That host with their banners at sunset were seen:
Like the leaves of the forest when autumn hath blown,
That host on the morrow lay withered and strown.

For the Angel of Death spread his wings on the blast,
And breathed in the face of the foe as he passed;
And the eyes of the sleepers waxed deadly and chill,
And their hearts but once heaved, and for ever
        grew still!

And there lay the steed with his nostril all wide,
But through it there rolled not the breath of his pride;
And the foam of his gasping lay white on the turf,
And cold as the spray of the rock-beating surf.

And there lay the rider distorted and pale,
With the dew on his brow, and the rust on his mail:
And the tents were all silent, the banners alone,
The lances unlifted, the trumpet unblown.

And the widows of Ashur are loud in their wail,
And the idols are broke in the temple of Baal;
And the might of the Gentile, unsmote by the sword,
Hath melted like snow in the glance of the Lord!

——∞∞∞——

Notes on selected words. *Fold*: sheepfold. *Cohorts*: group of soldiers. *Sheen*: shining surface. *Strown*: strewn; scattered. *Blast*: wind. *Waxed*: grew. *Steed*: horse. *Ashur*: an Assyrian city. *Unsmote*: unsmitten.

Commentary. The number of stories and poems that take their material straight from the Bible make up a small library. Sometimes the goal of these works is to make a biblical character or event come alive in our imaginations. Sometimes the author goes beyond this "presentational" level and aims to offer an interpretation or exegesis of the biblical passage. In doing one or both of these things, the author sometimes offers the work as an implied statement of personal belief in God and the Christian faith.

Byron's poem takes its substance from the narrative recorded in 2 Kings 19:35. When Sennacherib king of Assyria threatened to annihilate Judah and its king Hezekiah by besieging Jerusalem, God intervened by sending his angel at night and killing 185,000 soldiers in the Assyrian camp. When Sennacherib and other survivors "arose early in the morning" and beheld the dead bodies, they returned to their home country. The biblical account is a barebones record in a single verse. Byron amplified the few details into a full-fledged battlefield scene.

At the surface level, Byron's poem makes the biblical event come alive with imagined details. The key to the success of this inspired poem is twofold. One is the concrete imagery, much of it packaged in the form of similes. Everything is palpable in this poem, and the effects are both visual and aural (heard). The other masterful achievement is the galloping rhythm that sweeps us along. The metrical foot in this poem is anapestic—two unaccented syllables followed by an accented one. The forward sweep is helped along by an abundance of *and* coordinates at the beginnings of lines, in imitation of a feature of biblical style.

How do all these fireworks become devotional in nature? We enter into the event so completely that we cannot help but experience the excitement and drama of the destruction that God accomplished on an enemy nation. We experience the power and majesty of God, as well as his mercy in delivering his people from their enemy when their king prayed to God in the temple with Sennacherib's threatening letter laid open (2 Kings 19:14–19). The effect of the poem is doxological, leading us to praise God and be in awe of him.

Lines Written in Early Spring

WILLIAM WORDSWORTH (1770–1850)

I heard a thousand blended notes,
While in a grove I sat reclined,
In that sweet mood when pleasant thoughts
Bring sad thoughts to the mind.

To her fair works did Nature link
The human soul that through me ran,
And much it grieved my heart to think
What man has made of man.

Through primrose tufts, in that green
    bower,
The periwinkle trailed its wreaths;
And 'tis my faith that every flower
Enjoys the air it breathes.

The birds around me hopped and played,
Their thoughts I cannot measure,
But the least motion which they made
It seemed a thrill of pleasure.

The budding twigs spread out their fan,
To catch the breezy air;
And I must think, do all I can,
That there was pleasure there.

If this belief from heaven be sent,
If such be Nature's holy plan,

Have I not reason to lament
What man has made of man?

———⟨∞⟩———

Notes on selected words. *Reclined*: leaned backward against a support (such as a tree). *Primrose*: a species of flower. *Tufts*: clusters. *Periwinkle*: species of evergreen plant. *Do all I can*: obscure; perhaps a common saying that means "no matter what I might think to the contrary."

Commentary. Like several other poems in this anthology, this poem belongs to the realm of the literature of clarification and common experience. It takes only a step, however, to assimilate it as a devotional poem. The poem belongs to one of the oldest poetic genres of English literature. That genre is the reverdie—a poem written in praise of the coming of spring. While most members of this literary family are celebrations only, Wordsworth, in characteristic Romantic fashion, subjects his encounter with springtime nature to a process of meditation. The result is a type of poem that is virtually synonymous with Romantic nature poetry of the early nineteenth century—the meditative landscape poem.

The primary ingredient in the poem is the celebration of nature. We can profitably place Wordsworth's poem against a backdrop of nature psalms in the Old Testament. The nature psalms also celebrate nature, accepting it as a provision from God. They treat nature as a revelation from and about God, and Wordsworth too believes that nature imparts important information, saying that his meditation is a *belief* sent *from heaven*. Through many centuries of English literature, *heaven* was the default metonymy for God (a metonymy identifies a person or thing by means of something closely associated with it). Further religious imagery is associated with nature when Wordsworth ascribes a *holy plan* to it.

Many Romantic poets overrated nature in a way that Christians reject, but if we give Wordsworth the benefit of the doubt in this poem, we can join him in seeing the beautiful aspects of nature as a norm or standard by which to judge the corruption of human nature and civilization. In Jesus's discourse against anxiety (Matt. 6:25–34), Jesus too used nature as a norm by which to rebuke human striving, and in doing so he appealed to the same two aspects of nature that Wordsworth does in this poem—the birds of the air and the flowers of the field or woods.

Wordsworth's poem delivers a "good news" message and a "bad news" message. The good news is that nature as God created and intended it gives us a model for how to live. The bad news is *what man has made of man*. This is such a memorable saying that it became part of our storehouse of proverbs. A Christian reader can scarcely avoid making the connection to the Christian doctrine of the fall and its effects. Wordsworth is here leading us to meditate on a sad aspect of human experience in a fallen world. Wordsworth's magical phrase is as up-to-date as the daily news.

Earth Has Not Anything to Show More Fair

WILLIAM WORDSWORTH (1770–1850)

Earth has not anything to show more fair:
Dull would he be of soul who could
      pass by
A sight so touching in its majesty.
This City now doth, like a garment, wear
The beauty of the morning; silent, bare,
Ships, towers, domes, theaters, and
      temples lie
Open unto the fields, and to the sky,
All bright and glittering in the
      smokeless air.
Never did sun more beautifully steep
In his first splendor, valley, rock, or hill;
Ne'er saw I, never felt, a calm so deep!
The river glideth at his own sweet will.
Dear God! The very houses seem asleep;
And all that mighty heart is lying still!

Notes on selected words. *Fair*: pleasant to the eye. *Domes*: buildings with domes; Wordsworth particularly had in mind St. Paul's Cathedral, which is visible down the Thames River from Westminster

Bridge. *Temples*: churches; places of worship. *Steep*: cover or saturate. *Glideth*: glides.

Commentary. The published title of his sonnet alerts us to the place and occasion of its origin: "Composed upon Westminster Bridge, September 3, 1802." The phrase "composed upon" does not mean that Wordsworth actually composed the poem while seated on Westminster Bridge, which stands beside the Houses of Parliament in central London. The phrase means that he composed *upon the subject of* a morning scene at Westminster Bridge. The poem was composed in France a couple of days after the event that is recorded. Wordsworth and his sister Dorothy left London for the sea crossing at Dover in the early morning of September 3; Dorothy recorded the event in her journal, and Wordsworth in this famous sonnet.

Wordsworth's sonnet is permeated by religious language and feeling, making it easy for a Christian reader to assimilate it in a devotional way. What does the splendor of early morning mean to the soul? In the Bible, morning is viewed as a time of heightened spiritual awareness and openness to God. It is associated with worship, prayer, and revelation (as darkness is dispelled).

Structurally, this poem moves back and forth between an outpouring of feeling (lines 1–3, 9–11) and a description of the scene (4–8, 12–14). The opening line sets the tone, and everything after that is an expansion of that line. The key to everything in the poem is the early morning setting of the action. This is a city poem, but devoid of human activity. Wordsworth manages the description of the city scene in such a way as to make the city part of nature. Additionally, the imagery with which the poet paints the scene is so generalized that it could be virtually any beautiful city. One literary scholar calls the city in this poem a visionary city, speaking also of the purity of the unreal city. The imagery of the glittering sun and the buildings gleaming in its light, combined with the exalted and archaic language of the King James Bible, give the city a transcendent quality, an earthly emblem of the heavenly city of God. Psalm 46:4 comes readily to mind: "There is a river whose streams make glad the city of God."

To a Waterfowl

WILLIAM CULLEN BRYANT (1794–1876)

Whither, 'midst falling dew,
While glow the heavens with the last steps of day,
Far, through their rosy depths, dost thou pursue
Thy solitary way?

Vainly the fowler's eye
Might mark thy distant flight, to do thee wrong,
As, darkly seen against the crimson sky,
Thy figure floats along.

Seekest thou the plashy brink
Of weedy lake, or marge of river wide,
Or where the rocking billows rise and sink
On the chaféd ocean side?

There is a Power, whose care
Teaches thy way along that pathless coast,
The desert and illimitable air
Lone wandering, but not lost.

All day thy wings have fanned,
At that far height, the cold thin atmosphere,
Yet stoop not, weary, to the welcome land,
Though the dark night is near.

And soon that toil shall end,
Soon shalt thou find a summer home, and rest,
And scream among thy fellows; reeds shall bend,
Soon, o'er thy sheltered nest.

Thou art gone; the abyss of heaven
Hath swallowed up thy form, yet, on my heart
Deeply hath sunk the lesson thou hast given,
And shall not soon depart.

He who from zone to zone
Guides through the boundless sky thy certain flight,
In the long way that I must trace alone,
Will lead my steps aright.

———⧈———

Notes on selected words. *Whither*: where; to what destination. *Vainly*: futilely; without chance of success. *Fowler*: someone who hunts birds or wildfowl. *Plashy*: marshy; wet; waterlogged. *Brink*: edge. *Marge*: margin. *Billows*: large waves. *Chaféd*: rubbed, a reference to the motion of the ocean waves as they hit the shore. *A Power*: God; a divine being. *Illimitable*: boundless; without limits. *Abyss*: wide expanse; huge space. *He*: God. *From zone to zone*: everywhere; in all places. *Trace*: travel.

Commentary. The genre of this poem is the one that became dominant in the Romantic movement of the first half of the nineteenth century: the descriptive-meditative landscape poem. Also typical of the Romantic movement is the poet's turning what he sees in nature into a lesson for living. In this poem, that lesson focuses on God's providence in the lives of individuals.

This is an occasional poem: at age twenty-one, the author was walking from one New England town to another, seeking a place to settle as a lawyer. As night began to fall, he observed the flight of a bird as reconstructed in the poem. From start to finish, the poem is built on the technique known as apostrophe—addressing something or someone who cannot literally hear and respond but whom the poet addresses *as though* capable of hearing. The material falls into two subjects and focuses on two different "agents." One is the bird, with whom Bryant does two things. He first describes the flight of the bird (seemingly aimless but actually directed), and then he muses that the bird is headed for a resting place on the shore. Two stanzas shift the focus from the bird to God—the stanza in the middle that begins "There is a Power" and the final stanza. The action ascribed to God is providence, as God "teaches [the] way" of the bird's movement and "guides" the speaker.

The poem beautifully captures a teachable moment in the poet's life, and as readers we share that moment and can apply it to our lives. On the artistic side, the poem is written in the stanzaic form of the quatrain (*abab*), with a touch of originality in the fact that the first and last lines of each stanza are written in trimeter (three poetic feet, or six syllables), while the middle two lines are pentameter (five poetic feet, or ten syllables).

The Snow-Storm

RALPH WALDO EMERSON (1803–1882)

Announced by all the trumpets of the sky,
Arrives the snow, and, driving o'er the fields,
Seems nowhere to alight; the whited air
Hides hill and woods, the river, and the
      heaven,
And veils the farmhouse at the
      garden's end.
The sled and traveler stopped, the
      courier's feet
Delayed, all friends shut out, the
      housemates sit
Around the radiant fireplace, enclosed
In a tumultuous privacy of storm.

Come see the north wind's masonry.
Out of an unseen quarry evermore
Furnished with tile, the fierce artificer
Curves his white bastions with
      projected roof
Round every windward stake, or tree,
      or door.
Speeding, the myriad-handed, his
      wild work
So fanciful, so savage, nought cares he
For number or proportion. Mockingly,
On coop or kennel he hangs Parian
      wreaths;

A swan-like form invests the hidden thorn;
Fills up the farmer's lane from wall to wall,
Maugre the farmer's sighs; and at
    the gate
A tapering turret overtops the work.
And when his hours are numbered, and
    the world
Is all his own, retiring, as he were not,
Leaves, when the sun appears,
    astonished Art
To mimic in slow structures, stone by stone,
Built in an age, the mad wind's
    night-work,
The frolic architecture of the snow.

Notes on selected words. *Courier*: traveling messenger who rapidly carries urgent news. *Masonry*: the skillful work performed by a mason. *Artificer*: skilled craftsman. *Bastions*: outward-protruding parts of fortifications. *Windward*: facing toward the wind. *Nought*: nothing. *Coop*: cage for chickens. *Parian*: white marble. *Maugre*: despite. *Hours are numbered*: time is up. *Retiring, as he were not*: disappearing as if he did not even exist. *Mimic*: imitate. *Frolic*: playful.

Commentary. This poem belongs to the category of the literature of clarification and common experience rather than Christian affirmation. The author was not a professing Christian but a Romanticist in the nineteenth-century sense. Loosely speaking, we can say that a Romanticist ascribes to nature what a Christian ascribes to God. Yet "The Snow-Storm" is right on the borderland, just waiting for us to supply an element that enables us to read it in a devotional way.

Before we make that move, we should experience the poem on its own terms. This poem celebrates the power and artistry of a snow-storm. Emerson lived in rural, pre-urban New England at a time when winter was accompanied by paralyzing snowfalls. Living in such an environment, Emerson captures the essence of a snowstorm. The first stanza describes the arrival of the snow, which assaults the countryside with such suddenness and overwhelming quantity that it produces the situation that earlier eras called being snowbound. The effect of nature as portrayed in these lines is to subdue people and make them reverent toward the superior power of nature.

The second stanza describes what people see the next morning, after the snowstorm has departed. In Emerson's treatment, the landscape and farmstead become a stunning art display. The imagery comes from the human world of architecture and statues. The genius of these lines is that they enable us to see the effects of a heavy snowstorm in a new light and with a heightened awareness of the fantastic shapes left by the snow as it covers objects. Then in the last four lines the earlier word *mockingly* comes to fruition, as the poet draws our attention to the ability of the snowstorm to create art overnight that takes people a whole era to build.

It is easy to draw links between this poem and the Bible by ascribing to God what the poem ascribes to a force of nature. In Psalm 29, the song of the thunderstorm, God is pictured as the one who moves nature to perform its feats. Another nature psalm, Psalm 19, claims that nature shows God's "handiwork" (v. 1), which is exactly the right word for the artistry of Emerson's snowstorm. Psalm 147 catalogs God's easy control over nature (including the snow) and then asks, in a manner parallel to Emerson's poem, "Who can stand before his cold?" (v. 17). Emerson pictures snow as having an unseen quarry, and Job 38:22 pictures God as having storehouses of snow and hail. And so forth. A Christian reader of Emerson's poem is reminded of a Divine Being whom the poet does not name.

Strong Son of God, Immortal Love

ALFRED, LORD TENNYSON (1809–1892)

Strong Son of God, immortal Love,
　　Whom we, that have not seen thy face,
　　By faith, and faith alone, embrace,
Believing where we cannot prove:

Thine are these orbs of light and shade;
　　Thou madest life in man and brute;
　　Thou madest death; and lo, thy foot
Is on the skull which thou hast made.

Thou wilt not leave us in the dust:
　　Thou madest man, he knows not why,
　　He thinks he was not made to die;
And thou hast made him; thou art just.

Thou seemest human and divine,
　　The highest, holiest manhood, thou.
　　Our wills are ours, we know not how,
Our wills are ours, to make them thine.

Our little systems have their day;
　　They have their day and cease to be;
　　They are but broken lights of thee,
And thou, O Lord, art more than they.

We have but faith; we cannot know,
    For knowledge is of things we see;
    And yet we trust it comes from thee,
A beam in darkness; let it grow.

Let knowledge grow from more to more,
    But more of reverence in us dwell,
    That mind and soul, according well,
May make one music as before,

But vaster. We are fools and slight;
    We mock thee when we do not fear;
    But help thy foolish ones to bear;
Help thy vain worlds to bear thy light.

Forgive what seemed my sin in me,
    What seemed my worth since I began;
    For merit lives from man to man,
And not from man, O Lord, to thee.

Forgive my grief for one removed,
    Thy creature, whom I found so fair.
    I trust he lives in thee, and there
I find him worthier to be loved.

Forgive these wild and wandering cries,
    Confusions of a wasted youth;
    Forgive them where they fail in truth,
And in thy wisdom make me wise.

Notes on selected words. *Orbs*: orbits, meaning the planets. *Madest*: made. *Brute*: animal. *Thy foot is on the skull*: you are Lord over death; you have vanquished death. *Seemest*: are seen to be. *Our little systems*: our merely human systems of belief. *As before*: before science and secularism undermined belief in Christianity; a reference to the religious doubt of the Victorian age. *Slight*: of small importance. *Vain* *worlds*: corrupt and empty human worlds. *Bear*: carry; bear witness to. *One removed*: Arthur Henry Hallam, Tennyson's close friend who died at the age of twenty-two. *These wild and wandering cries, Confusions of a wasted youth*: my elegiac poems mourning the death of Hallam.

Commentary. Tennyson composed this poem as the prologue to his long work entitled *In Memoriam*, a collection of 131 lyric poems written as an extended elegy about the death of his friend Arthur Henry Hallam. The prologue was composed last and stands as a statement of the belief at which Tennyson arrived after struggling with religious doubt in some of the poems that make up *In Memoriam*. This context makes this strong assertion of belief even more moving.

In form, the poem is an extended prayer addressed to Christ, the Son of God. The content of the poem falls into place readily if we apply the normal ingredients of prayer, as follows: an exalted opening invocation to Christ; five stanzas of praise (with each stanza praising Christ for a specific act or attribute); two stanzas of petition; three stanzas asking Christ for forgiveness. Two themes are intermingled throughout the poem: an expression of faith in Christ and his strength, and acknowledgment of the weakness and inadequacy of people. Although the poem is written in a short and simple stanzaic form known as "the *In Memoriam* stanza" (quatrains rhyming *abba*), that simplicity is played off against a dignified and high style for which Tennyson is known.

The poem is a notable expression of faith in an unseen spiritual reality that cannot be proven empirically. *We have but faith*, the poet declares halfway through. The opening stanza puts into words what John 20:24–29 and Hebrews 11 assert about faith as opposed to sight. From this stance of believing something beyond the earthly and human, the poem becomes a magnificent statement of submission and resignation to a higher being and reality.

Crossing the Bar

ALFRED, LORD TENNYSON (1809–1892)

Sunset and evening star,
    And one clear call for me!
And may there be no moaning of the bar,
    When I put out to sea,

But such a tide as moving seems asleep,
    Too full for sound and foam,
When that which drew from out the boundless
      deep
    Turns again home.

Twilight and evening bell,
    And after that the dark!
And may there be no sadness of farewell,
    When I embark;

For though from out our bourne of Time and Place
    The flood may bear me far,
I hope to see my Pilot face to face
    When I have crossed the bar.

Notes on selected words. *One clear call*: the bell that signals the departure of a ship from a harbor. *Moaning of the bar*: mournful sound of water passing over a sand bar at the mouth of a harbor at low tide.

Seems asleep: is calm; this line and the next picture the tide as being so high that it moves imperceptibly and without commotion over the sandbar, thereby allowing safe passage of the boat as well. That which drew from out the boundless deep turns again home: two meanings are in view: (1) the incoming high tide drew water up from the ocean, and then the water returns "home" to where it came from as the tide goes out, and (2) the speaker's soul will return to its supernatural home when he passes from life to death (pictured as a vast unknown ocean). Bourne: boundary. Pilot: God.

Commentary. Tennyson wrote this poem on the back side of a used envelope during a twenty-nine-minute boat crossing from the English mainland to the Isle of Wight on which he lived. Tennyson had recently recovered from a serious illness and was eighty years old. He said that the poem "came in a moment." A few days before his death, Tennyson expressed the wish that this poem would always be printed last in all editions or collections of his poetry. The poem was sung at his funeral in Westminster Abbey.

Along with Milton's sonnet on his blindness (see page 129), this is the most famous poem of resignation in the English language. The implied situation in the poem, which is also the universal human experience embodied, is that of a person contemplating his death and what lies beyond it. The poem is built around a single controlling metaphor in which the speaker's passage from life to death is pictured as a ship's departure from a harbor into the ocean at twilight. The crucial point in that passage is a sandbar, and the speaker's prayer is that the tide will be so high that the ship can make the passage easily.

This poem draws upon a conventional motif known as the forbidding of sorrow on an occasion that would ordinarily induce it. The poem derives its power partly from the mood of calm resignation and partly from the universal archetypes that operate powerfully in it. These include life as a journey; death as a vast, unknown sea; God as a pilot who guides; the end of life as sunset, twilight, darkness, and home; facing death alone; saying goodbye; the sorrowing survivor. On the artistic side, the verse form is one of the poem's perfections: the rhyme scheme of abab carries through all the stanzas, but the line lengths of each stanza are different.

In the Bleak Midwinter

CHRISTINA ROSSETTI (1830–1894)

In the bleak midwinter, frosty wind made moan,
Earth stood hard as iron, water like a stone;
Snow had fallen, snow on snow, snow on snow,
In the bleak midwinter, long ago.

Our God, Heaven cannot hold Him, nor earth sustain;
Heaven and earth shall flee away when He comes
       to reign.
In the bleak midwinter a stable place sufficed
The Lord God Almighty, Jesus Christ.

Enough for Him, whom cherubim, worship night
       and day,
Breastful of milk, and a mangerful of hay;
Enough for Him, whom angels fall before,
The ox and ass and camel which adore.

Angels and archangels may have gathered there,
Cherubim and seraphim thronged the air;
But His mother only, in her maiden bliss,
Worshiped the beloved with a kiss.

What can I give Him, poor as I am?
If I were a shepherd, I would bring a lamb;
If I were a Wise Man, I would do my part;
Yet what I can I give Him: give my heart.

Notes on selected words. *Ass*: donkey (archaic). *I would do my part*: would bring a gift that corresponds to my position as a wise man; perhaps the implication is that the speaker would bring one of the gifts that Matthew 2:11 records as gifts from the wise men who visited the infant Jesus.

Commentary. This is a Victorian Christmas poem, written by a poet who wrote some two hundred religious lyrics. The description of the bleak midwinter setting whisks us away in our imaginations not to Bethlehem but to Britain. The impact of the poem depends on the poet's evocation of the commemoration of Christ's birth as Christians have observed it in England and America for centuries.

The most memorable parts of the poem are the strong opening line and the strong concluding line. A good approach toward analysis of the poem is to follow the process by which Rossetti moves from the first line to the last one. The opening stanza focuses on the midwinter theme, doing a magnificent job of making us nearly shiver with cold. This initial movement serves two purposes: it leads us to imagine our own remembered Christmas times, and it establishes the world into which Jesus was born as an inauspicious world, seemingly unworthy of the Christ child. A long tradition of devotional contemplation would label the opening stanza "composing the scene," but the original twist here is that this stanza composes the scene of an English Christmas rather than an event from the Bible.

After lines 5–6 remind us of the exalted status of Jesus and his coming again in power and glory, stanzas 2–3 set up a countermovement: that the bleak earthly surroundings were, paradoxically, sufficient for Jesus at his birth. The fourth stanza is a transition designed to set up the poem's conclusion: although the grand angelic hosts attended the birth of Jesus, only the humble mother of Jesus worshiped the infant Jesus with human affection. The concluding stanza is as striking as the opening one. It is structured as a problem that requires a solution, namely, what the speaker (and we with her) can offer as an appropriate gift to the Christ child. The surprise ending sounds the authentic note of Christian submission.

This simple piety is embodied in a poem that in its form, too, is based on the principle of simplicity. The rhyme scheme is couplets (consecutive lines that end with rhyming words). A mother's milk and manger of hay are said to suffice for the king of kings. The acts that matter most are a mother's kiss and the gift of a humble person's heart.

Good Friday

CHRISTINA ROSSETTI (1830–1894)

Am I a stone and not a sheep
That I can stand, O Christ, beneath thy cross,
To number drop by drop Thy blood's slow loss,
And yet not weep?

Not so those women loved
Who with exceeding grief lamented thee;
Not so fallen Peter weeping bitterly;
Not so the thief was moved;

Not so the sun and moon
Which hid their faces in a starless sky,
A horror of great darkness at broad noon—
I, only I.

Yet give not o'er,
But seek thy sheep, true Shepherd of the flock;
Greater than Moses, turn and look once more
And smite a rock.

Notes on selected words. *Those women*: the women who stood within sight of the cross when Jesus was crucified. *I, only I*: the implied meaning is that only the speaker is unmoved by the sight of Jesus's crucifixion. *Give not o'er* ["over"]: do not give up on; do not consign to the unbelieving segment of the world.

Commentary. This is a subtle poem in which the first three stanzas gradually build a tension that reaches a breaking point in the packed last stanza. The point of unity in the first three stanzas is the speaker's self portrait of being unmoved by the spectacle of Jesus's crucifixion. The speaker emerges as the archetypal outsider, ignominiously out of step with the sorrow that other people and even nature showed when Jesus was crucified. Even though the speaker does not respond with appropriate grief, the very pictures that the poem paints lead the reader to sorrow for the dying Christ. The imagery of the opening line—*stone* and *sheep*—are a subtle set-up for the memorable last stanza.

The first three stanzas are the speaker's self-address, but in the last stanza the poet turns in prayer to Christ. Having implicitly declared herself to be a failure in the Christian walk, the speaker asks for a rescue operation. The prayer draws upon three separate biblical reference points. The first is Jesus as the Good Shepherd who seeks and saves his lost sheep. The second is Moses, a supreme hero of the Old Testament and yet someone regarding whom Christ is declared superior in two famous New Testament passages (John 1:17; Heb. 3:1–6). The climactic prayer—to be smitten by Christ and subdued by him—draws upon Peter's denial of Jesus. On that occasion, Jesus is said to have "turned and looked at Peter" (Luke 22:61), leaving Peter convicted. Further, the name "Peter" means rock, so (as the last line has it) Jesus can be said to have smitten Peter with his look, and additionally Moses smote the rock in the wilderness.

The devotional potential of the poem is at least two-pronged. One is to move us to the grief that we should feel when confronted with the details of Jesus's suffering for our sins. The second lesson is that following Jesus requires that we repent of what is lacking in us and be submissive to Jesus. As we live with this poem, it gradually emerges as a confession and plea for forgiveness.

Up-Hill

CHRISTINA ROSSETTI (1830–1894)

Does the road wind up-hill all the way?
   Yes, to the very end.
Will the day's journey take the whole long day?
   From morn to night, my friend.

But is there for the night a resting-place?
   A roof for when the slow dark hours begin.
May not the darkness hide it from my face?
   You cannot miss that inn.

Shall I meet other wayfarers at night?
   Those who have gone before.
Then must I knock, or call when just in sight?
   They will not keep you standing at that door.

Shall I find comfort, travel-sore and weak?
   Of labor you shall find the sum.
Will there be beds for me and all who seek?
   Yea, beds for all who come.

Notes on selected words. *Travel-sore*: exhausted and worn out from travel. *Find the sum*: reach the right conclusion; find final satisfaction.

Commentary. This poem falls into a familiar literary family known as poems with two voices. The rhyme scheme of *abab* accentuates this, and the poem as printed above follows an optional editorial practice of placing the answers to the questions in italics. The question and answer format lends a childlike quality, with the ongoing series of questions reflecting the anxieties and uncertainties to which children are prone and regarding which they do not hesitate to ask questions. The questioner is a traveler, and the answering voice is a guide. There are eight questions and eight answers. Underlying the entire poem are two powerful archetypes. The first is life as a journey and its end an arrival at a final destination. The second is a lifetime as a day, ending in night.

This poem is one for which we can say that "context is everything." The literary world at large places the poem into a context of Victorian doubt and interprets it as a poem of stoicism bordering on despair. In such a context, life consists of a wearying uphill climb, with the traveler being continually prodded on by a vague promise of eventual rest (which, however, seems a very long way off). Secondly, this poem appears in a number of anthologies of children's literature. Within that context, the images of rest, night, and bed fit right into a child's experience, and no deeper meanings are sought beyond assurances of security.

In religious circles, the poem is interpreted as a poem about heaven. On this reading, the questions raised by the traveler paint a realistic picture of the difficulties of earthly life. We should give this half of the equation its due weight because the title of the poem puts the focus on life as an arduous up-hill climb. The answers can be viewed as coming from Jesus or the voice of Christian truth rooted in the Bible and Christian theology about life and its heavenly destination. The language and images of the poem somewhat continuously echo phrases from the Bible, and the whole poem can be viewed as an elaboration of Jesus's statement to his disciples in John 14:2: "In my Father's house are many rooms. . . . I go to prepare a place for you."

Pied Beauty

GERARD MANLEY HOPKINS (1844–1889)

Glory be to God for dappled things—
For skies of couple-color as a brinded cow;
For rose-moles all in stipple upon trout that swim;
Fresh-firecoal chestnut-falls; finches' wings;
Landscape plotted and pieced—fold, fallow, and
      plough;
And all trades, their gear and tackle and trim.

All things counter, original, spare, strange;
Whatever is fickle, freckled (who knows how?)
With swift, slow; sweet, sour; adazzle, dim;
He fathers-forth whose beauty is past change:
                         Praise him.

Notes on selected words. *Dappled*: ordinarily it means spotted, or having spots of different color from the background, but in view of how this poem develops, perhaps it has the more general meaning of being variegated rather than uniform. *Brinded*: having streaks; more generally, made up of more than one color. *Rose-moles*: colored spots, in this case on a trout fish. *In stipple*: a pattern constructed out of small dots. *Fresh-firecoal chestnut-falls*: at the very least, this is a picture of freshly fallen chestnuts on the grass beneath the tree;

the image seems to telescope out from that to the practice of roasting chestnuts, causing the nuts to split open, with the inside differing in color from the shell. *Plotted and pieced*: divided into fields of various shapes. *Fold*: enclosure for animals, such as a sheepfold. *Fallow*: land that has been plowed but left unsown for a season. *Plough*: a plowed field. *Trades*: equipment belonging to various activities such as fishing and sailing (as examples). *Adazzle*: bright; glittering. *Fathers-forth*: begets; brings into existence; perhaps also demonstrates the qualities of a father.

Commentary. This brief but packed poem is an "encomium"—a poem that praises either a character type (such as the virtuous wife of Proverbs 31:10–31) or an abstract quality (such as love in 1 Corinthians 13). This poem praises the artistic quality of variety, or being variegated rather than uniform. The British particularly love this aesthetic quality and (for example) prefer a flowerbed consisting of many different flowers and colors instead of a single species or color. Additionally, whereas the expansive landscapes of America tend toward big fields or vistas of the same thing, the landscapes of England are small and pieced irregularly. In addition to being an encomium, this poem is a brief psalm of praise to God, in the mode of the psalms of praise in the Old Testament.

Before we look further at the content of this poem, we need to note some features of Hopkins's poetic techniques. Hopkins was an innovator. He loved to make up new words and pack his poems with unusual images drawn from obscure areas of life. He also specialized in original and far-fetched metaphors, similes, and analogies. Finally, sound effects were a high priority with Hopkins. The result is a "fireworks" type of poetic style.

In "Pied Beauty," Hopkins compressed as many images as possible of objects of differing colors, shapes, and textures. Some of his images are references to specific animals or plants, and elsewhere he uses abstract words to name general categories—swift and slow, for example. The poet's goal is twofold. On the one hand, he wants to awaken us to an artistic quality of everyday life so we can enjoy it. Secondly, he wants us to experience this beauty of nature as a manifestation of God, thereby transmuting artistic enjoyment into spiritual adoration of God. The poem begins and ends as the nature poems in the book of Psalms do—by praising God. The next-to-last line also does this, and in contrast to all of the variety and change that the poem has shown to exist in nature, God is said to be transcendent above such cyclic reality, being *past change*. The simple two-word doxology (command to praise) of the last line provides closure to the poem and is also a simple contrast to the dazzling imagery of the preceding poem.

Spring

GERARD MANLEY HOPKINS (1844–1889)

Nothing is so beautiful as Spring,
When weeds, in wheels, shoot long and lovely and lush;
Thrush's eggs look little low heavens, and thrush
Through the echoing timber does so rinse and wring
The ear, it strikes like lightnings to hear him sing;
The glassy pear tree leaves and blooms, they brush
The descending blue; that blue is all in a rush
With richness; the racing lambs too have fair their fling.
What is all this juice and all this joy?
A strain of the earth's sweet being in the beginning
In Eden garden. Have, get, before it cloy,
Before it cloud, Christ, Lord, and sour with sinning,
Innocent mind and Mayday in girl and boy,
Most, O maid's child, thy choice and worthy
       the winning.

Notes on selected words. *Weeds*: probably plants generally; Hopkins wanted a word starting with *w* to form alliteration with *wheels*. *Wheels*: circles. *Look*: look like (an implied simile). *Timber*: forest. *Rinse and wring the ear*: completely fill the ear with a commotion of sound. *Have fair their fling*: are unhindered in their jumping and romping. *Cloy*: become unpleasant through excess of sweetness. *Mayday*:

the happiness and high spiritedness associated with Mayday celebrations. *Maid's child*: Jesus, child of the virgin Mary.

Commentary. From time immemorial, nature has provided poets with a "language" for writing on a wide range of subjects. Love poetry, for example, is filled with nature imagery, with the Song of Solomon being a notable example. The result is that when poets write a meditative nature poem it is often impossible to know from the first half of the poem what turn the poem will take as it concludes. In George Herbert's poem "Virtue" (see page 90), three stanzas on the subject of the transience of nature give way to a final stanza to the unexpected subject of the immortality of the virtuous soul. Hopkins's poem on spring follows a similar path. The poem is an Italian sonnet in which the octave describes the beauty of spring, and then the sestet moves by way of transition to a prayer addressed to Christ on an unanticipated subject.

The first item on Hopkins's agenda is to create a riot of sensations in our imaginations as a way of capturing the exuberance of nature in springtime. Hopkins loves to use words in original ways and to create a "fireworks" of sound effects. Those two factors are always capable of "trumping" an easy flow of meaning, so we need to take the time to analyze how the words (which may have been chosen for sound effects) are appropriate to the content. To relish the poet's creativity is always an avenue to appreciating a work of literature.

Two further developments then emerge in the second part of the poem. First Hopkins introduces the thought (conventional in literature) that the beauty of nature is an echo or remembrance of God's original paradise, the garden of Eden. With associations of innocence thus established, the poem becomes a prayer addressed to Christ, asking him to win innocent children to belief in him before sin draws them away to a life of unbelief. The interweaving of references is skillfully accomplished (as always in Hopkins), and we might note that Jesus is himself identified as "maid's child."

The devotional application of this poem is threefold. The description of spring becomes a hymn of praise for God's creation. Secondly, paradise is a master image of the Christian imagination, and longing for its qualities has a therapeutic spiritual effect on the human psyche. Thirdly, the poem focuses our attention on our children and grandchildren and the youthful generation in our home church, and on their need to be claimed for the faith while they are young.

The Windhover

To Christ Our Lord

GERARD MANLEY HOPKINS (1844–1889)

I caught this morning morning's minion, king-
dom of daylight's dauphin, dapple-dawn-drawn Falcon, in
    his riding
Of the rolling level underneath him steady air; and striding
High there, how he rung upon the rein of a wimpling wing
In his ecstasy! Then off, off forth on swing,
As a skate's heel sweeps smooth on a bow-bend: the hurl
    and gliding
Rebuffed the big wind. My heart in hiding
Stirred for a bird,—the achieve of, the mastery of the thing!
Brute beauty and valor and act, oh, air, pride, plume, here
Buckle! AND the fire that breaks from thee then, a billion
Times told lovelier, more dangerous, O my chevalier!
No wonder of it: sheer plod makes plough down sillion
Shine, and blue-bleak embers, ah my dear,
Fall, gall themselves, and gash gold-vermilion.

—⦵—

Notes on selected words. *Windhover*: kestrel, a species of falcon (*hover* should be pronounced as we pronounce it as a verb). *Minion*: medieval term of royalty, referring to one highly favored. *Dauphin*: another term of royalty, referring to the heir apparent to the French throne. *Dapple*: varicolored. *Dawn-drawn*: drawn to activity by the dawn. *Rolling level underneath him steady*: the phrase *underneath him* points both backward to *rolling level* and forward to *steady*: although the air is turbulent or *rolling*, the bird so masters it that underneath him it is both level and steady. *Rung upon the rein*: circled, with the reference being to the process of breaking in a horse by making it circle around the trainer at the end of a long (e.g., twenty-foot) rein. *Wimpling*: rippling or flapping. *On swing as a skate's heel sweeps smooth on a bow-bend*: after rising in a spiral manner, the bird glides horizontally the way an ice skater sweeps over the ice in a figure-eight or curving motion. *Hurl and gliding*: a summary of the two motions that have been described— rising vertically into the wind and then gliding horizontally. *Rebuffed*: pushed back; mastered; controlled. *My heart in hiding*: the speaker's hidden position from the bird. *Act*: action. *Air*: impressive appearance (from which we get our common saying "putting on airs"). *Plume*: possibly plumage or feathers of a bird, but more likely a continuation of regal terms preceding it and therefore meaning royal splendor of garments. *Buckle*: the primary meaning is fall or plummet downward, submitting to the wind; secondary meaning of join, fasten, or fuse, since the qualities named in the preceding line join the bird and its motion. *More dangerous*: more powerful; more to be feared by the prey for which the bird is plummeting. *Chevalier*: knight, the third term of medieval royalty that has been applied to the bird. *Sheer plod makes plough down sillion shine*: the sheer act of the horses' plodding forward, pulling the plow behind them, makes the furrow and/or the plowshare shine. *Gall*: perhaps rub; the picture is that of the embers falling through the grate and hitting the metal as they do so. *Gash*: split open. *Vermillion*: brilliant red color.

Commentary. Several genres converge in this poem: it is a sonnet divided into an octave and sestet, each with its own subject matter; it is a descriptive-meditative poem; and it belongs to a category of nature poetry known as the morning walk. The poem is dedicated to Christ, though this dedication was added long after the poem was composed. The poem is Hopkins's "signature poem," and he regarded it as his best poem, which may explain why he belatedly dedicated it to Christ his Lord.

At the first level, the poem is a nature poem that celebrates the beauty and mastery of a kestrel, a species of hawk or falcon. The whole poem turns on the action of the bird in first mastering the turbulent morning wind and then submitting to it. The bird is said to be even more impressive when it submits to the wind than when it masters it. Hopkins believed that everything in the universe has its own differentiating, unique quality, which he called *inscape*. The inscape of the bird that this descriptive poem captures is strength that stoops to conquer. The supreme example of this is the incarnation of Jesus and his death on the cross. The poem subtly pushes us in this direction with the dedication after the title and the imagery of the last line (*gall* and *gash*, which figure in the gospel account of Jesus's crucifixion).

God's Grandeur

GERARD MANLEY HOPKINS (1844–1889)

The world is charged with the grandeur of God.
It will flame out, like shining from shook foil;
It gathers to a greatness, like the ooze of oil
Crushed. Why do men then now not reck his rod?
Generations have trod, have trod, have trod;
And all is seared with trade; bleared, smeared with toil,
    with toil,
And wears man's smudge and shares man's smell;
    the soil
Is bare now, nor can foot feel, being shod.
And for all this, nature is never spent;
There lives the dearest freshness deep down things;
And though the last lights off the black West went,
Oh, morning, at the brown brink eastward, springs—
Because the Holy Ghost over the bent
World broods with warm breast and with ah!
    bright wings.

Notes on selected words. *Charged*: as used here, this word has three simultaneous meanings: energized; pushing or attacking forward, as in an army's charge; carrying a burden, or charged with a responsibility. *Shook foil*: gold foil (or our more familiar aluminum foil) off of which light glints when it is turned or shaken. *Oil*: oil crushed from a plant, such as olives. *Reck*: heed, from which the opposite *reckless* comes. *Seared*: scorched or burned. *Bleared*: made dim. *Nor can foot feel, being shod*: an allusion to the story of Moses at the burning bush (Ex. 3:5), where Moses is told to remove his sandals because the ground on which he is standing is holy ground. *Spent*: depleted; exhausted. *Deep down things*: there is an ellipsis, and the meaning is deep down *in* things. *Brink*: horizon. *Bent world*: round, but also morally and spiritual crooked, or deviating from a straight or "upright" standard.

Commentary. The subject of this sonnet is the permanent freshness that nature possesses: no matter what the human race does to exhaust nature, it remains perpetually resilient and living. The interpretive slant that Hopkins gives to this phenomenon of nature is the assertion that it declares God's grandeur or greatness. The poem is thus a nature poem that becomes a psalm of praise, even ending with a specifically theological statement about the Holy Spirit in his role as Creator.

The poem is organized on a three-part, envelope principle. The first four lines celebrate what might be called God's nature. The question that concludes this unit is actually a transition to the middle section, which describes the ways in which the human race does not reck or heed God's rule. Lines 5–8 describe humankind's "nature," that is, their exploitation of nature and failure to nurture it. The last six lines then return to God's nature, declaring that the creative power of the Holy Spirit makes nature indestructible.

As with other Hopkins's poems, this one requires that we take the time to unpack the meanings of the individual images. Verbal effects like internal rhyme within a line and alliteration (repetition of initial sounds in words located close to each other) enliven the effect.

O World Invisible, We View Thee

FRANCIS THOMPSON (1859–1907)

O world invisible, we view thee;
O world intangible, we touch thee;
O world unknowable, we know thee;
Inapprehensible, we clutch thee!

Does the fish soar to find the ocean,
The eagle plunge to find the air,
That we ask of the stars in motion
If they have rumor of thee there?

Not where the wheeling systems darken,
And our benumbed conceiving soars!—
The drift of pinions, would we hearken,
Beats at our own clay-shuttered doors.

The angels keep their ancient places:
Turn but a stone and start a wing!
'Tis ye, 'tis your estrangéd faces,
That miss the many-splendored thing.

But (when so sad thou canst not sadder)
Cry—and upon thy so sore loss
Shall shine the traffic of Jacob's ladder
Pitched betwixt Heaven and Charing Cross.

Yea, in the night, my Soul, my daughter,
Cry—clinging to Heaven by the hems;
And lo, Christ walking on the water,
Not of Genesareth, but Thames!

∞∞∞

Notes on selected words. *Soar*: fly upward. *Wheeling*: turning or rotating. *Systems*: solar systems or galaxies. *Not where the wheeling systems darken, And our benumbed conceiving soars*: probably a contrast to the next two lines—angels are right around our bodies, not in the far-off galaxies. *Pinions*: angels' wings. *Clay-shuttered doors*: our human minds and bodies, on the premise that humans were originally made from dust or clay; these are shuttered in the sense of being oblivious to the angels around them. *Charing Cross*: a famous intersection in the center of London. *Genesareth*: the Sea of Galilee, on which Jesus once walked. *Thames*: the River Thames, which flows through London.

Commentary. For the record, this poem bears the titles "The Kingdom of God" and "In No Strange Land" in various editions. The poem is one of the great assertions of the immanence of God—his presence within his creation. At the same time, it instructs us in the need to exercise faith in the unseen spiritual world as the vehicle by which we can experience the closeness of God in his creation and our everyday lives. Several biblical passages function as sub-texts for this poem. One is Hebrews 11:1: "Now faith is . . . the conviction of things not seen." Another is verse 6 of that same chapter: "Whoever would draw near to God must believe that he exists and that he rewards those who seek him." A third is 1 Peter 1:8: "Though you do not now see him, you believe in him." This poem is built on the idea that believing is seeing, in reversal of the common saying that seeing is believing.

The poem unfolds in three movements. Stanza one is a series of four paradoxes, each of one which asserts that by faith we can experience the invisible spiritual world. It is only to the external senses that the spiritual world is *invisible, intangible, unknowable*, and *inapprehensible*. 1 Corinthians 2 asserts this same viewpoint, claiming at one point that "what no eye has seen, nor ear heard . . . God has revealed to us through the Spirit" (vv. 9–10). Stanzas 2–4 then assert in multiple ways that it is human unbelief that renders the spiritual world closed to human experience; the spiritual world itself is present for any who exercise faith in it.

The final two stanzas then bring the theme of immanence onto "center stage." The poet has the boldness to locate Jacob's ladder (Gen. 28:12–16) not in Palestine but at a busy London intersection, and Christ walking on the water not on the Sea of Galilee but the Thames River in London.

A Prayer in Spring

ROBERT FROST (1874–1963)

Oh, give us pleasure in the flowers today;
And give us not to think so far away
As the uncertain harvest; keep us here
All simply in the springing of the year.

Oh, give us pleasure in the orchard white,
Like nothing else by day, like ghosts by night;
And make us happy in the happy bees,
The swarm dilating round the perfect trees.

And make us happy in the darting bird
That suddenly above the bees is heard,
The meteor that thrusts in with needle bill,
And off a blossom in mid air stands still.

For this is love and nothing else is love,
To which it is reserved for God above
To sanctify to what far ends he will,
But which it only needs that we fulfill.

—⟨⟩—

Notes on selected words. *Nothing else by day*: seen directly as they
are, in contrast to how they might appear (for example, as ghosts) at
night. *Dilating*: making wider or larger. *Meteor*: metaphor for "the

darting bird" of line 9. *Needle bill*: thin beak, also called bill. *This*: the antecedent is vague, but perhaps it can be inferred to be the pleasure and happiness that have been the subject of the first three stanzas; alternatively, the implied antecedent is something like *nature*.

Commentary. The complexity of this ostensibly simple poem (written in couplets) becomes apparent if we relate it to its multiple literary genres. The poem praises the coming of spring and therefore belongs to a very old and esteemed genre known as the reverdie. Because the praise of spring is placed in a religious framework, the poem is akin to the psalm of praise. And the title correctly identifies the poem as a prayer, enabling us to infer that God is the one who is addressed in the petitions of the first three stanzas.

At its simplest level, the poem is a description of the sights of nature in springtime. In successive stanzas, the poem allows us to vicariously experience the flowers, the orchard with its bees, and the hummingbird hovering above a flower and thrusting its thin beak into it. As an overlay on this descriptive level, the poem evokes a feeling of pleasure and happiness (with the words *pleasure* and *happy* both appearing two times). The world of nature is abuzz with life; the prayer is that people might be attuned to that same life force and joy.

Then, as an additional overlay, the final stanza turns the experience in a spiritual direction, and the poem becomes a theological statement. First the life force of nature is said to be love. God is declared to be the one who sanctifies love for his own purposes. But a human responsibility is then added to the mix, as people are declared the ones who fulfill God's ends of sanctification. All of this requires pondering and application.

Journey of the Magi

T. S. ELIOT (1888–1965)

"A cold coming we had of it,
Just the worst time of the year
For a journey, and such a long journey:
The ways deep and the weather sharp,
The very dead of winter."
And the camels galled, sorefooted, refractory,
Lying down in the melting snow.
There were times we regretted
The summer palaces on slopes, the terraces,
And the silken girls bringing sherbet.
Then the camel men cursing and grumbling
and running away, and wanting their liquor and women,
And the night-fires going out, and the lack of shelters,
And the cities hostile and the towns unfriendly
And the villages dirty and charging high prices:
A hard time we had of it.
At the end we preferred to travel all night,
Sleeping in snatches,
With the voices singing in our ears, saying
That this was all folly.

Then at dawn we came down to a temperate valley,
Wet, below the snow line, smelling of vegetation;
With a running stream and a water-mill beating the darkness,
And three trees on the low sky,
And an old white horse galloped away in the meadow.
Then we came to a tavern with vine-leaves over the lintel,

Six hands at an open door dicing for pieces of silver,
And feet kicking the empty wine-skins.
But there was no information, and so we continued
And arriving at evening, not a moment too soon
Finding the place; it was (you might say) satisfactory.

All this was a long time ago, I remember,
And I would do it again, but set down
This set down
This: were we led all that way for
Birth or Death? There was a Birth, certainly
We had evidence and no doubt. I had seen birth and death,
But had thought they were different; this Birth was
Hard and bitter agony for us, like Death, our death.
We returned to our places, these Kingdoms,
But no longer at ease here, in the old dispensation,
With an alien people clutching their gods.
I should be glad of another death.

Notes on selected words. *The magi*: the wise men who traveled to visit the infant Jesus. *Quotation marks surrounding the first five lines*: these lines are a nearly verbatim quotation from a Christmas sermon by the Renaissance Anglican preacher Lancelot Andrewes. *Galled*: in pain. *Refractory*: stubborn or unmanageable. *Dispensation*: society with its institutions and procedures.

Commentary. When poets take their content from the Bible, they do as many as three things: (1) they make the biblical event come alive in our imagination; (2) they offer an interpretation of the biblical event; and (3) by means of those two things they express their personally held Christian beliefs. Eliot does all three things in this poem, which was the first poem in which he demonstrated his Christian faith after publicly announcing his conversion. In the last stanza the poem becomes a conversion poem.

This poem was part of a "Christmas card" series authored by contemporary poets and published in the late 1920s by the publishing house (Faber and Faber) for which Eliot worked as an editor. Whereas the conventional Christmas card treats the journey of the wise men sentimentally, Eliot's poem presents a consistent bleakness and leads us to see the sacrificial purpose of Christ's coming to earth. As we analyze the life that the wise man lives upon his return to his pagan society back home, we are given a sobering reminder of what it means to become a Christian.

Even though the poem narrates the story of one man, it embodies a universal human experience, namely, searching for Jesus and following him after finding him. The form into which Eliot cast this experience is known as the dramatic monologue—a speech addressed to an implied listener. The speaker is one of the wise men in old age, and he here reminisces before an unidentified person who is taking notes (see the opening lines of the last stanza). The wise man's words combine narration and reflection. Each stanza is distinctively different from the others. The first stanza uses the techniques of realism to narrate the physical and psychological hardships of the journey. The second stanza uses conventional Christian symbolism and biblical allusions to establish the sacrificial nature of Christ's coming. In the third stanza the wise man interprets his experience. If we read these lines carefully, we see that the speaker is now a Christian believer for whom the *Death* (capitalized) of Christ was *our death* (a substitutionary death). Life with an *alien people* is so difficult that the speaker would be *glad of another death*, that is, for earthly death as the gate to life (as Milton termed it). The wise man's experience is every believer's experience.

Two Poems on Death and Immortality

EMILY DICKINSON (1818–1884)

The Bustle in a House

The Bustle in a House
The Morning after Death
Is solemnest of industries
Enacted upon Earth—

The Sweeping up the Heart
And putting Love away
We shall not want to use again
Until Eternity—

Because I Could Not Stop for Death

Because I could not stop for Death—
He kindly stopped for me—
The Carriage held but just Ourselves—
And Immortality.

We slowly drove—He knew no haste
And I had put away
My labor and my leisure too,
For His Civility—

We passed the School, where Children strove
At Recess—in the Ring—
We passed the Fields of Gazing Grain—
We passed the Setting Sun—

Or rather—He passed Us—
The Dews drew quivering and Chill—
For only Gossamer, my Gown—
My Tippet—only Tulle—

We paused before a House that seemed
A Swelling of the Ground—
The Roof was scarcely visible—
The Cornice—in the Ground—

Since then—'tis Centuries—and yet
Feels shorter than the Day
I first surmised the Horses' Heads
Were toward Eternity—

Notes on selected words. *Industries*: tasks. *Civility*: politeness; graciousness; the general meaning is that Death is a winsome visitor and chauffeur. *Gossamer*: thin fabric. *Tippet*: scarf. *Tulle*: thin silk. *Cornice*: ornamented molding just below a ceiling—in other words, near the top of a room or building; what is being described is a grave.

Commentary. In reading the poems in this anthology, we can scarcely miss the point of how often the poets have written poems that lead us to meditate on the process of dying. Emily Dickinson lived in a New England village in an era when many death scenes occurred in people's homes. Living close to death, Dickinson was preoccupied with it in her poems. In terms of religious conviction, Dickinson is an elusive figure, and her poems express the whole range of sentiments from doubt to faith. The two poems printed above assume an afterlife and can be read devotionally, though they do not show a specifically Christian allegiance.

"The Bustle in a House" situates us in a house the morning after someone has died in it. The action is domestic—bustling about a house, sweeping the floor, and putting things away. These actions are metaphoric for what surviving loved ones experience when the deceased has left their lives. Cessation of relationship is the keynote, as the survivors get on with their lives without the deceased person in the house. The element of faith resides in the certainty of hope that the poem asserts about reunion in eternity.

"Because I Could Not Stop for Death" also domesticates the act of dying by treating it as a leisurely carriage drive through the countryside. A personified Death is the chauffeur. Initially the ride is pleasant. As the moments toward actual death approach, the sun sets and the air grows cold. The final stop is before a grave. The poem unfolds as a riddle (for which Dickinson is famous in her poems), and not until the final two stanzas do we fully realize that the speaker is talking to us from the afterlife.

A Latin motto from the classical past was *respice finem*—"consider your end." It is important to be ready for death when it comes and not leave this life in a panic. Poems such as these two by Emily Dickinson can help us to be realists by impressing on us that our death is inevitable and that we can prepare ourselves for it. These poems can also help us toward acceptance of the death of loved ones.

Nature as God's Revelation

The Marshes of Glynn
Sidney Lanier (1842–1881)

As the marsh-hen secretly builds on the watery sod,
Behold I will build me a nest on the greatness of God.
I will fly in the greatness of God as the marsh-hen flies
In the freedom that fills all the space 'twixt the marsh and
    the skies.
By so many roots as the marsh-grass sends in the sod
I will heartily lay me ahold on the greatness of God.
Oh, like to the greatness of God is the greatness within
The range of the marshes, the liberal marshes of Glynn.

Frost at Midnight
Samuel Taylor Coleridge (1772–1834)

But thou, my babe, shalt wander like a breeze
By lakes and sandy shores, beneath the crags
Of ancient mountain, and beneath the clouds,
Which image in their bulk both lakes and shores
And mountain crags; so shalt thou see and hear
The lovely shapes and sounds intelligible
Of that eternal language, which thy God
Utters, who from eternity doth teach
Himself in all, and all things in himself.
Great universal Teacher! He shall mold
Thy spirit, and by giving make it ask.

Commentary. Both of these passages are brief excerpts from longer poems. Sidney Lanier's poem ranks as regional writing because its subject matter comes from a specific locale, namely, the salt marshes of Glynn County in coastal Georgia. "The Marshes of Glynn" appears in an unfinished collection of nature lyrics entitled *Hymns of the Marshes*. These nature poems are a religious testament as well as nature writing. The famous stanza on the marsh-hen expresses a lesson that the poet draws from a creature of nature, thereby leading us to meditate on how nature is a revelation in our own lives as well as a personal testimony by the poet.

The theme of the stanza is the greatness of God, a phrase that appears four times. Additionally, the poet asserts his resolve to personally take possession of the greatness of God in his life. The teachers that prompt him to this resolve are multiple. Seeing the hen's nest on the sod suggests the act of building security on God. The flight of the hen in the expanse of the sky prompts the thought of living in the greatness of God. And the spectacle of the marsh grass sending its roots into the sod leads to a resolve to lay hold on the greatness of God.

The situation within Coleridge's poem is the poet's watching his infant son in a cradle at midnight on a winter night in rural England. The poem is structured as the random association of ideas that went through the poet's mind. Coleridge remembered his own upbringing in London, where his only experience of nature was the sky and stars. That leads to the passage printed here, in which the ecstatic father contrasts his urban upbringing to what he foresees as his son's childhood in a natural setting. The exalted language of the passage magnifies nature as a master teacher who is ultimately God.

The devotional effect of these passages is to give us a model for looking to nature as God's book from which we can learn how to conduct our lives.

Sunday Worship

For Sunday
Christopher Smart (1722–1771)

> Arise, arise, the Lord arose
> On this triumphant day.
> Your souls to piety dispose;
> Arise to bless and pray.
>
> Even rustics do adorn them now,
> Themselves in roses dress;
> And to the clergyman they bow
> When he begins to bless.
>
> Their best apparel now arrays
> The little girls and boys,
> And, better than the preacher, prays
> For heaven's eternal joys.

The Rime of the Ancient Mariner
Samuel Taylor Coleridge (1772–1834)

> O Wedding-Guest! This soul hath been
> Alone on a wide wide sea:
> So lonely 'twas, that God himself
> Scarce seeméd there to be.
>
> O sweeter than the marriage-feast,
> 'Tis sweeter far to me,
> To walk together to the kirk
> With a goodly company!

To walk together to the kirk,
And all together pray,
While each to his great Father bends,
Old men, and babes, and loving friends
And youths and maidens gay!

Farewell, farewell! But this I tell
To thee, thou Wedding-Guest!
He prayeth well, who loveth well
Both man and bird and beast.

He prayeth best, who loveth best
All things both great and small;
For the dear God who loveth us,
He made and loveth all.

———⊶⊷———

Notes on selected words. *Dispose*: incline. *Rustics*: farmers. *In roses*: wearing roses as decoration. *Better than the preacher prays*: the "Sunday best" clothing of the children prays better than the preacher with his prayers from the pulpit. *Kirk*: church. *Gay*: colorfully dressed.

Commentary. A poem by George Herbert titled "Sunday" (see page 108) is a meditation on the spiritual meaning of Sunday for the believing soul. The two poems printed above offer quaint descriptions of the social or communal dimension of Sunday observance in a bygone age. These pictures are still an option for Christians today.

Christopher Smart's short poem devotes an opening stanza to the spiritual blessings of Sunday observance, and then two stanzas to the physical appearance of worshipers that sets Sunday apart from the other days of the week. Behind this picture lies a principle that once dominated people's thinking about Sunday, namely, that people's physical appearance signals the importance they attach to the event for which they have dressed. Working the other way, people's attitudes and behavior rise or sink to the level at which they dress. Smart's poem pictures people being called to their higher selves by making Sunday special.

The stanzas from Coleridge's "The Rime of the Ancient Mariner" come at the end of the poem, which narrates the mariner's fall into sin followed by redemption from the effects of his sin. The mariner here addresses the wedding guest who has been the unwilling audience of his recounted journey into isolation through a crime against nature. These stanzas represent the mariner's final wisdom learned from his journey into sin and redemption. This makes Coleridge's picture of Sunday all the more significant. The good life of the forgiven soul is what Coleridge called "the One Life"—a life lived in union with God, people, and nature. And what is the best picture that Coleridge could find to embody this vision? Neighbors flocking to church on Sunday to pray. In the middle stanza of the excerpt, the word *together* appears three times in three successive lines.

Christmas Day

Rejoice and Be Merry
Anonymous (medieval)

> Rejoice and be merry in song and in mirth!
> O praise our Redeemer, all mortals of earth!
> For this is the birthday of Jesus our King,
> Who brought us salvation—His praises we'll sing!

This Is the Month
John Milton (1608–1674)

> This is the month, and this the happy morn,
> Wherein the Son of Heaven's eternal King,
> Of wedded maid and virgin mother born,
> Our great redemption from above did bring;
> For so the holy sages once did sing,
> That he our deadly forfeit should release,
> And with his Father work us a perpetual peace.
>
> That glorious form, that light unsufferable,
> And that far-beaming blaze of majesty,
> Wherewith he wont at Heaven's high council-table
> To sit the midst of Trinal Unity,
> He laid aside, and, here with us to be
> Forsook the courts of everlasting day,
> And chose with us a darksome house of mortal clay.

Notes on selected words. *This* [line 1 of Milton's poem]: the way is left open for the reference to be to (1) the literal day of Christ's birth, (2) the year Milton wrote his nativity ode (1629), and (3) any subsequent Christmas day. *The holy sages*: the Old Testament prophets. *Forfeit*: penalty; loss of a right. *Glorious form*: Christ's divine person, exalted in heaven. *Unsufferable*: too intense to be endured by humans, a reference to 1 Timothy 6:16, which tells us that God "dwells in unapproachable light, whom no one has ever seen or can see." *Wont*: accustomed. *Midst*: in the middle of. *Trinal Unity*: the triune Godhead. *Darksome house of mortal clay*: physical human body.

Commentary. The first excerpt is the opening stanza of a medieval Christmas poem discovered in an old church gallery book in Dorset, England.

The implied setting of both poems is Christmas Day, as the day's ceremonies are set to get under way. The first poem epitomizes the simplicity of the medieval folk imagination. It states the essentials and lets it go at that. The exuberance is what counts, and the poem packs its punch with its exclamations and emotive vocabulary. Additionally, a heavy incidence of anapestic feet (two unaccented syllables followed by an accented one, to form a three-syllable foot rather than the customary two-syllable one) keeps the pace lively. Technically the poem is a doxology or command to praise God.

Milton's poem is the opposite of those stylistic traits. The two stanzas are the opening of Milton's exalted ode titled "On the Morning of Christ's Nativity" (known to literary scholars as "Milton's nativity ode"). If the medieval poem captures the naïve innocence of an era when life was simple, Milton's stanzas belong to the Baroque (embellished) style of the Renaissance. The exalted style embodies the exaltation of the incarnation.

Both of Milton's stanzas employ the syntax (sentence arrangement) known as a suspended sentence, meaning that we reach the main subject and verb only after extensive preliminary subordinate clauses. In the first stanza, the main sentence element comes in line 4. In the second stanza, it comes in line 5. Long syntax like this is a feature of the high style. Another feature of that style is the prevalence of epithets—titles for persons and things, such as *the Son of Heaven's eternal King* as a title for Christ, and *the holy sages* for the Old Testament prophets.

Despite the contrasting styles of the two poems, the subject of both is the same: not the nativity or birth but the theological meaning of that event—the incarnation, not a baby in the manger. The operative words are thus *salvation* and *redemption* and related terms such as *release* and *perpetual peace*.

Nature as a Religious Experience

WILLIAM WORDSWORTH (1770–1850)

It Is a Beauteous Evening

It is a beauteous evening, calm and free;
The holy time is quiet as a nun
Breathless with adoration; the broad sun
Is sinking down in its tranquility;
The gentleness of heaven broods o'er
  the sea.
Listen! The mighty Being is awake,
And doth with his eternal motion make
A sound like thunder—everlastingly.

Tintern Abbey

  Therefore am I still
A lover of the meadows and the woods
And mountains, and of all that we
  behold
From this green earth, of all the mighty
  world
Of eye, and ear . . . ;
  well pleased to recognize
In nature and the language of the sense
The anchor of my purest thoughts,
  the nurse,

The guide, the guardian of my heart,
    and soul
Of all my moral being. . . .
Knowing that nature never did betray
The heart that loved her; 'tis her
    privilege,
Through all the years of this our life,
    to lead
From joy to joy: for she can so inform
The mind that is within us, so impress
With quietness and beauty, and so feed
With lofty thoughts, that neither evil
    tongues,
Rash judgments, nor the sneers of
    selfish men,
Nor greetings where no kindness is,
    nor all
The dreary intercourse of daily life,
Shall e'er prevail against us, or disturb
Our cheerful faith, that all which we
    behold
Is full of blessings.

Notes on selected words. *Beauteous*: beautiful. *Broods o'er*: hovers over. *Language of the sense*: sensations. *Nurse*: could be either a mother who sustains the life of a suckling infant or a medical nurse who restores to health; both would fit Wordsworth's view of what nature does in a person's life. *Intercourse of daily life*: the interactions that make up a typical day's events. *E'er*: ever.

Commentary. The religious stance of the Romantic poets of the nineteenth century is complex. These poets were people of religious sensibility, but their doctrinal convictions were only partly Christian. By Christian standards, these poets often claim too much for nature, even viewing it as divine. Between the extremes of indiscriminately claiming these poets to be Christian in viewpoint and wholesale rejection of what they wrote lies a middle road that Augustine metaphorically called "raiding the Egyptians" (an allusion to how the Israelites left Egypt laden with treasures that were pressed upon them by the Egyptians, who were eager to get the Israelites out of the country). For purposes of devotional reading, we can segregate out the excessive claims made for nature and concentrate on passages such as those excerpted above. We do not want to claim that nature is divine, but we *do* want to experience God in nature, and the passages such as these can help us do so.

The first passage is from a sonnet belonging to the genre known as the evening walk. This particular evening walk is on the sea coast. The language in the lines is religious and is fed by Christian and biblical sources. We do not know whether the "Being" that Wordsworth senses in the scene is the Christian God or a pantheistic spirit in nature, but for Christians it is God.

The second excerpt is from a major poem with such a long title that literary scholars simply call it "Tintern Abbey." Like the sonnet excerpted above, this poem is an occasional poem. It took its origin from Wordsworth's revisiting the ruins of Tintern Abbey on the bank of the Wye River in Wales. The lines printed here perform three tasks. The first is to affirm the beauty and healing power of nature. Second, at the beginning of the second verse paragraph, Wordsworth makes large claims for *nature and the language of the sense* [sensations] because he believed that all of our knowledge and morality is formed by the images and sensations that we absorb, and not from innate ideas that are ours at birth. We do not need to accept that doctrine entirely in order to agree with Wordsworth that the quality of our thinking, feeling, and morality is influenced by whether we take in good images or cheap and depraved ones.

Finally, as the passage keeps unfolding, Wordsworth expresses a *cheerful faith* in the benevolence of the universe in our lives. We can read this as a parallel to Paul's great statement that "for those who love God all things work together for good" (Rom. 8:28).

The Consolations
of Providence

From *Samson Agonistes*
John Milton (1608–1674)

> All is best, though we oft doubt,
> What the unsearchable dispose
> Of highest wisdom brings about,
> And ever best found in the close.
> Oft he seems to hide his face,
> But unexpectedly returns
> And to his faithful champion hath in place
> Bore witness gloriously. . . .
> His servants he with new acquist
> Of true experience from this great event
> With peace and consolation hath dismissed,
> And calm of mind all passion spent.

From *Hamlet*
William Shakespeare (1564–1616)

> Our indiscretion sometime serves us well
> When our deep plots do pall, and that should
>   learn us
> There's a divinity that shapes our ends,
> Rough-hew them how we will. . . .
>
> There is a special providence in the fall of
>   a sparrow.
> If it be now, 'tis not to come;

if it be not to come, it will be now;
if it be not now, yet it will come;
the readiness is all.

Notes on selected words. *Dispose*: disposal; outcome. *Highest wisdom*: God and his providence. *His faithful champion*: Samson. *Acquist*: acquisition. *This great event*: Samson's pulling down the temple on the worshipers of Dagon. *Indiscretion*: mistakes. *Deep plots*: elaborate plans. *Pall*: fail. *Learn*: teach. *A divinity*: God. *Shapes our ends*: molds our destiny. *Rough-hew*: carve or chip a statue in its early, unfinished or unpolished stage of composition. *It*: the reference in these three lines is to death. *The readiness is all*: the most important thing is to be ready to act when the opportunity arises.

Commentary. These passages are the final moments of epiphany (insight or revelation) in the works in which they appear, making the sentiments about providence even more important than they would otherwise be. The first passage is the final choral speech in Milton's closet drama *Samson Agonistes*. The lines from *Hamlet* are Hamlet's moment of transformation that enables him to perform his final act before dying.

Milton's play recreates the tragic story of Samson. The stance is retrospective in the sense that when the play opens Samson has already made his tragic decisions and is being punished for them. Milton went beyond the story told in Judges 13–16 and composed a full-fledged account of the hero's spiritual regeneration. The tragic action ends with the death of Samson brought about by his pulling down the temple of Dagon on the pagan Philistines. The final speech in the play, excerpted here, is expressed by the chorus—the ideal audience who represents us as well. In the circuitous workings of God's providence through seemingly tragic events, the mystery of divine providence asserts itself. The response is acceptance of a pattern that is now completed with the death of the protagonist. This is one of the uses of the doctrine of providence: posthumous understanding and contentment (*calm of mind*). It is an appropriate sentiment at a funeral.

Shakespeare's tragic hero Hamlet lives a life similar to Milton's Samson. Until the very end of the play, Hamlet makes a mess of nearly everything he undertakes. Seeing the corruption of his society (the court of Denmark), he undertakes singlehandedly to set things right. At last he recognizes the futility of such human overreaching and is ready to wait for God's providence to give him the opportunity to perform his destined work of bringing a murderer (King Claudius) to judgment. The first excerpt pictures God as a divine sculptor who overrides the blunders that people make in their lives. The reference to the sparrow in the second excerpt comes from Matthew 10:29–31, Jesus's discourse on trusting God and not fearing the threats of the world. In *Hamlet*, the consolation of providence occurs in a context of impending future action. The drift of Hamlet's thinking is that since no one can control the time of his death—since only God in his providence knows that—we should put fear aside and be ready to boldly accomplish God's purposes in the world. Although the clause *the readiness is all* refers at a secondary level to readiness for death when it comes, in the context of Shakespeare's play the primary meaning is to be ready for action (even dangerous action that might lead to death) as God's providence arranges it.

Certainty of Faith

No Coward Soul Is Mine
Emily Brontë (1818–1884)

No coward soul is mine,
No trembler in the world's storm-troubled sphere;
I see Heaven's glories shine,
And Faith shines equal, arming me from fear.

O God within my breast,
Almighty, ever-present Deity,
Life that in me hast rest,
As I, undying life, have power in thee,

Vain are the thousand creeds
That move men's hearts, unutterably vain,
Worthless as withered weeds
Or idlest froth amid the boundless main,

To waken doubt in one
Holding so fast by thy infinity,
So surely anchored on
The steadfast rock of immortality.

I Never Saw a Moor
Emily Dickinson (1830–1886)

I never saw a moor,
I never saw the sea;
Yet know I how the heather looks,
And what a wave must be.

> I never spoke with God,
> Nor visited in heaven;
> Yet certain am I of the spot
> As if the chart were given.

Notes on selected words. *O God within my breast* . . . : the syntax in this stanza is very difficult; the approach taken is to treat the entire second stanza as a direct address to God, with the next two stanzas representing what the speaker says to God after this extended address. *As I, undying life*: having asserted in the preceding line that life resides within her, the speaker now clams to *be* undying life. *Vain*: futile; having no effect. *Thousand creeds*: not Christian creeds but creeds of unbelief that might instill doubt in a weak Christian. *Main*: the sea or main body of water, in contrast to the weeds and froth along its sides. *Chart*: map.

Commentary. Biographical context makes these testimonies of faith even more memorable than they would otherwise be. According to Emily Brontë's sister Charlotte, "No Coward Soul Is Mine" was the last thing that Emily wrote before her death. It is part of a spiritual quickening that Emily underwent in the days preceding her death from tuberculosis at the age of thirty. Furthermore, according to tradition, Emily Dickinson requested that "No Coward Soul Is Mine" be read at her funeral.

The theme of Brontë's poem is double. The references to seeing *Heaven's glories shine* in line 3 and to *immortality* in the last line of this excerpt pushes the line of thought in the specific direction of the Christian's afterlife in heaven. If we combine that with the possible deathbed context of the poem, it becomes easy to read the whole poem as a statement of faith in immortality. In fact, it helps explain the opening emphasis on courage, inasmuch as it takes courage not to fear (line 4) when facing physical death. But the poem expresses certainty of conviction in life as well as death. It is a testament of faith for living in a "storm-troubled sphere" as well as facing death. We should note that the speaker continuously asserts her faith against enemies such as fear and doubt. She presents herself as engaged in a single combat against foes who want to destroy her faith.

Emily Dickinson's poem is cut from the same cloth as Brontë's poem. It too expresses confidence of faith in an unseen spiritual world and the God who resides there. The main technique is that of analogy: just as the speaker can know what a moor and ocean are like without having literally seen them, so she can believe in God without having spoken to him and in heaven without having visited there. Whereas the Brontë poem is filled with conflict, Dickinson's poem is serene.

What joins the two poems is their tone. There is an "all out" quality to both assertions of faith. We sense that the voice of doubt would be wasting its time trying to convert these two souls.

Our Only Secure Home

ANONYMOUS (DATE UNKNOWN)

Conclusion of *The Wanderer*

Everything is troublesome in the earthly kingdom;
The turn of events changes the world under heaven.
Here wealth is fleeting, here friends are fleeting,
Here man is fleeting, here family is fleeting.
The whole foundation of the earth turns to emptiness.

So spoke the wise man in his spirit as he sat alone
    with his thoughts.
Good is the one who keeps his faith. . . .
It will be well for him who seeks mercy,
Consolation from the father in heaven, where all
    security stands for us.

Conclusion of *The Seafarer*

God established the rocky foundations,
the solid surface of the earth and the heavens above.
Foolish is the one who does not fear the Lord;
    death will find him unprepared.
Blessed is the one who lives humbly; mercy comes
    to him from heaven.
The Maker makes him firm in heart because he
    believes in His might. . . .
Let us consider where we have a home,
and then think about how we may come there;
and let us also strive to reach that place

244

of eternal blessedness,
where life is to be found in the love of the Lord,
hope in heaven. Thanks be to the Holy One,
who bestows honor on us, the Lord of Glory,
Eternal Lord, for all time. Amen.

Commentary. These passages about our true home in heaven are moving in themselves, but they assume even more depth when we know something about their context. The two poems excerpted above (and translated from the Old English by Leland Ryken) are similar in nature and belong to a tradition of Old English poetry known as the "elegiac tradition." They are not elegies in the sense of being funeral poems but in the more general sense of lamenting the insecurity of earthly life and institutions. Funeral elegies end by expressing consolation in the form of hope of immortality in heaven. Both poems are built around the meditation of a protagonist who is an exile from former security and is now enduring a solitary sea voyage through an icy seascape. As these two tragic figures take stock of their loss and isolation, they gradually move toward a Christian consolation. Contrary to what secular scholars say, these conclusions are not "tacked on" but are instead the inevitable conclusion toward which both poems have headed from the beginning.

Two motifs give shape to the passages printed above. The first is the acknowledgment (only hinted at in the second passage but abundantly evident in the poem as a whole) that earthly life provides no lasting security for a person. Both poets seek to spare us from misplaced trust, and they therefore express a warning to us. The antidote to false trust is the second motif in the passages. That motif is the admonition to place our trust for permanent security in God and the hope of heaven. This is elemental, bedrock Christianity, and it is a fitting conclusion to this anthology.

Biographical Notes

Abelard, Peter. French monk who lived 1079–1142. He was most famous as a scholar and theologian; in those roles he had a high regard for literature and poetry.

Addison, Joseph. Neoclassical (late seventeenth and early eighteenth centuries) man of letters; best known as an essayist.

Blake, William. An eccentric poet and artist, Blake was a forerunner of the Romantic movement of the early nineteenth century. He was not an orthodox Christian but incorporated much from the Bible into his poetry and art.

Bradstreet, Anne. Seventeenth-century Puritan New England poet; the first important poet of the New World.

Brontë, Emily. British author of mid-nineteenth century; best known for her only published novel, *Wuthering Heights*.

Bryant, William Cullen. A nineteenth-century American poet of the Romantic movement.

Byron, Lord (George Gordon Byron). A poet of the English Romantic movement of the early nineteenth century. Notorious for his profligate lifestyle, Byron nonetheless composed some beautiful lyrics and religious poems that Christians can endorse, especially a volume entitled *Hebrew Melodies*.

Caedmon. A farmhand at Whitby Abbey in northwest England in the seventh century. He is the first poet of the English tradition, composing in the language known as Anglo-Saxon or Old English. His ability to compose poetry came as a sudden and direct endowment from God.

Chatterton, Thomas. Chatterton, who committed suicide at the age of seventeen, is best known for a hoax in which he passed off his own poetry as material written by a fifteenth-century author.

Coleridge, Samuel Taylor. Along with William Wordsworth, a leading light of the early Romantic movement in England.

Constable, Henry. A late sixteenth century English poet with Catholic convictions.

Dickinson, Emily. A leading American poet of the second half of the nineteenth century. Her specialty was short lyric poems with original twists.

Donne, John. Donne (1573–1631) was a poet by avocation; his primary vocation was that of an Anglican preacher as Dean of St. Paul's Cathedral. He became one of the most famous preachers of English ecclesiastical history. His poetry is voluminous, being divided between love poetry and religious poetry.

Dryden, John. A professional man of letters of the Restoration (late seventeenth century) who helped establish new directions in literature known as neoclassicism.

Eliot, T. S. (Thomas Stearns Eliot). A towering figure of twentieth-century literature, and one of the most important and influential Christian writers of the modern era.

Emerson, Ralph Waldo. An American essayist and poet who was a leading disseminator of Romantic thought in the middle of the nineteenth century.

Francis of Assisi. Italian Catholic friar who lived 1181–1226.

Frost, Robert. One of the most famous twentieth-century American poets.

Herbert, George. Although he was raised in privileged aristocratic circles, in his mid-thirties he turned his back on political prominence and became an Anglican priest in a small rural parish near Salisbury. On his deathbed at the age of forty, he turned over a volume of devotional poems entitled *The Temple*, which was published posthumously in 1633.

Herrick, Robert. A seventeenth-century poet and Anglican cleric who wrote over 2,500 poems, mainly on the subject of romantic love.

Hopkins, Gerard Manley. A Roman Catholic poet and Jesuit priest of the Victorian era. His poetic style was not that of Victorianism such as Tennyson wrote; instead he wrote in isolation in a style that helped forge the modern (twentieth-century) poetic idiom, a situation that accords with the fact that his poetry was published posthumously in 1918.

Jonson, Ben. A Renaissance poet and playwright, and a contemporary of Shakespeare, Donne, and Herbert. He was secular in orientation and wrote only a few religious poems.

Lanier, Sidney. Nineteenth-century America poet and literary scholar.

Milton, John. A seventeenth-century Puritan poet and scholar. As Latin Secretary to Cromwell, Milton was one of the most famous public figures of his day. Despite being many-talented, Milton regarded poetry as his primary life's calling. *Paradise Lost* is his major work and was written after he became blind at the age of forty-four.

Pope, Alexander. The leading English poet of the neoclassic era (first half of the eighteenth century).

Revius, Jacob. Dutch poet and Calvinist theologian. He wrote in the metaphysical style of John Donne and George Herbert, of whom he was a contemporary.

Rossetti, Christina. Victorian poet of the nineteenth century. Her religious views were those of high church Anglicanism infused with evangelical fervor.

Shakespeare, William. The most famous English writer of all time, known primarily for his plays but also as the author of a 154-poem sonnet collection. He belongs to the Renaissance period of English literature (late sixteenth and early seventeenth centuries).

Sidney, Sir Philip. A mid-sixteenth century English Renaissance poet and statesman. As a poet, he is primarily known for a sequence of love sonnets entitled *Astrophil and Stella*. He was known in his day as a champion of Protestantism.

Smart, Christopher. Eighteenth-century English poet.

Spenser, Edmund. One of the greatest English poets, he wrote in many genres and is best known for a narrative romance in poetic form entitled *The Faerie Queene*. He lived in the second half of the sixteenth century, and his religious convictions were Protestant leaning toward Puritanism.

Taylor, Edward. New England Puritan poet and minister of the late seventeenth and early eighteenth centuries. He wrote in the metaphysical style of John Donne and George Herbert.

Tennyson, Alfred, Lord. The major Victorian poet. The total corpus of his poetic output is astounding, and it is often rooted in the traditions of the past, including Christianity.

Thompson, Francis. Late Victorian poet who led a tortured life of poverty, illness, and addiction.

Traherne, Thomas. Seventeenth-century metaphysical poet and Anglican clergyman.

Vaughan, Henry. Seventeenth-century Welsh physician and metaphysical poet who was especially influenced by the poetry of George Herbert.

Wordsworth, William. The most important English Romantic poet (first half of the nineteenth century). He possessed a religious temperament, but often this found expression in a religion of nature rather than Christian orthodoxy. His poetry is saturated with the influence of the King James Bible and references to Christian doctrine.

Sources and Acknowledgments

The purpose of this bibliographic essay is to explain where the poems reprinted in this anthology came from, and where relevant to credit publishers who hold the copyright to texts.

Nearly all of the poems reprinted in this anthology are pre-twentieth-century texts that are in the public domain. No publisher owns a copyright to these works. Instead, they belong to everyone as a shared possession. It is true that when publishing companies republish these texts, they themselves copyright their books, but this should not be construed to mean that they own the copyright to the texts they have republished. These companies are in the same position as I find myself as editor of this anthology: they are the beneficiaries of a common text that they are privileged to pass on to their readers.

Multiple Internet sites explain copyright and public domain guidelines. The most helpful one is the Cornell University Library copyright information center. Other sites list poems in the public domain, and these include "Public Domain Poetry" and "Christian Poetry in the Public Domain" (part of the website of Utmost Christian Writers).

In compiling this anthology, I have been in quest for a common text of individual poems. This shared text lies behind every modern reprinting of it. I myself picture this common text as floating "out there," waiting to be claimed.

How does one gain access to this common text? I will provide a brief personal narrative of how it has happened for me. Most of the poems I have reprinted are ones that I have taught over the course of half a century as a college professor of English. These poems appear in typed or Xeroxed form in my class notes. Where did I find them? I do not know precisely, but many of them came from two anthologies that were my "bread and butter" resources first encountered as a student, namely, *The Norton Anthology of English Literature* (two volumes, published by W. W. Norton and Company in 1962), and a companion two-volume anthology of American literature dating from the same era. An additional two-volume anthology of American literature was *American Poetry and Prose*, ed. Norman Foerster (Boston: Houghton Mifflin, 1957).

Equally foundational for me were anthologies that covered individual eras of English literature: *Seventeenth-Century Prose and Poetry*, ed. Frank J. Witherspoon and Alexander M. Warnke (Harcourt, 1963); *Anthology of Romanticism*, ed. Ernest Bernbaum (John Wiley, 1948); and *Victorian Poetry and Poetics*, ed. Walter E. Houghton and G. Robert Stange (Houghton Mifflin, 1959).

All of these anthologies gave me access to the commonly possessed version of the poems that I have printed in this anthology, but none of the publishers of the anthologies owns the copyright to the poems. Instead, each publisher disseminated the poems as shared common property.

Today when I turn to the task of assembling a poem that I am about to teach or include in a published work, I am inclined to turn to the Internet. When I type the title of a famous poem into a search engine, I immediately have access to multiple sites that carry the poem. I compare versions from these sites and quickly codify a teaching or publishing version of the poem. Postings on the Internet have often done what I have done in this anthology, namely, modernize the spelling, punctuation, and formatting with the goal of clarifying the poem for a modern reader. The resulting version of a poem can be called eclectic, meaning that it does not necessarily reproduce a specific published or posted version. I myself think of the resulting poem as coming in some way from all of the published or posted versions. Internet sites do not assign poems in the public domain to a publisher because no publisher owns the copyright.

From the foregoing global perspective, I am ready to turn to a more specific account of the origin, preservation, and dissemination of the poems that appear in this anthology. The list that follows consists mainly of the books where individual poems were first published, including a few books still under copyright.

The Old English and Middle English poems survived in the form of handwritten manuscripts that came to reside in university libraries.

For the texts that I used in composing my translations of these poems, I used Internet versions of the original Old and Middle English poems. In the process of composing my translations, I did what translators always do (and what I observed as a member of the translation committee of the English Standard Version): I paid attention to what various translators did with the text, I was influenced by them, but I did not duplicate what any one of them had done.

The publication information for the remaining medieval selections is as follows. Peter Abelard's poem "O What Their Joy and Their Glory Must Be" was translated by famed Victorian hymn translator John Mason Neale and was first published in *Hymnal Noted* (1854); "Canticle of the Sun" by Francis of Assisi was translated by Benen Fahy and printed in *St. Francis of Assisi: Writings and Early Biographies*, ed. Marion A. Habig (Chicago: Fanciscan Herald Press, 1973); the opening stanza of "Rejoice and Be Merry" was taken from *The English Carol Book, Second Series* (London: A. R. Mowbray and Company, 1913).

In selecting poems from eras after the Middle Ages, I followed the eclectic approach described above. I did not consult the books where the poems were originally published, but listing those sources will be instructive and interesting in itself. For the sixteenth and seventeenth centuries, the list is as follows. Sir Philip Sidney's "Leave Me, O Love": *Certain Sonnets* (1598); Edmund Spenser's sonnet: *Amoretti and Epithalamion* (1595); Henry Constable's sonnet: *Diana: The Sonnets and Other Poems of Henry Constable* (1859); the sonnets by Shakespeare: *Shakespeare's Sonnets* (1609); Shakespeare's *Hamlet: First Folio* (1623); "Yet If His Majesty": *Lyrics from the Song Books* (1888); John Donne's sonnets: *Holy Sonnets* (1633); poems by George Herbert: *The Temple* (1633); Ben Jonson's nativity poem: *Poems from the Second Folio* (1641); Milton's nativity ode, "On Time," and Sonnet 7: *Poems of Mr. John Milton* (1645); remaining Milton sonnets: *Poems* (1673); *Paradise Lost* (1667, 1674); *Samson Agonistes: Paradise Regained . . .* (1671); two poems by Robert Herrick: *Noble Numbers* (1648); Anne Bradstreet: *The Tenth Muse, Lately Sprung up in America* (1650); Thomas Traherne's "Poverty": *The Poetical Works of Thomas Traherne* (1903); Henry Vaughan: *Silex Scintillans* (1650); John Dryden's ode: *To The Pious Memory of the Accomplish'd Young Lady Mrs. Anne Killigrew* (1686); Dryden's hymn translation: *Examen Poeticum* (1693).

The copyright information for the sonnet by Dutch poet Jacob Revius is as follows: "He Bore Our Griefs," translated by Henrietta Ten Harmsel in *Jacob Revius: Selected Poems*, published by Wayne State University Press of Detroit in 1968. Used by permission of Wayne State University Press.

The publication facts for the eighteenth-century poems are as follows: Joseph Addison's two poems appeared in the literary periodical *The Spectator* in 1712; Alexander Pope's "The Dying Christian to His Soul": *The Spectator*, 1712; the two poems by Edward Taylor: *The Poems of Edward Taylor*, ed. Donald E. Stanford (New Haven: Yale University Press), 1960; Thomas Chatterton: *The Poetical Works of Thomas Chatterton* (1795); Christopher Smart, "For Sunday": *Hymns for the Amusement of Children* (1771).

The Romantic movement of the late eighteenth and early nineteenth centuries yields the following list: William Blake: "The Lamb" in *Songs of Innocence* (1776), and "And Did Those Feet" in *Milton: A Poem* (1808); Lord Byron's "The Destruction of Sennacherib": *Hebrew Melodies* (1815); William Wordsworth: "Lines Written in Early Spring" in *Lyrical Ballads* (1798), and two sonnets in *Poems, in Two Volumes* (1807); Samuel Taylor Coleridge, "Frost at Midnight" and "The Rime of the Ancient Mariner": *Lyrical Ballads* (1798); William Cullen Bryant: *Poems* (1821); Ralph Waldo Emerson, "The Snow-Storm": *Poems* (1847); all of the poems by Emily Dickinson: *Poems* (1890) and *Poems: Second Series* (1891); Sidney Lanier, "The Marshes of Glynn": *Hymns of the Marshes* (1882); Emily Brontë, "No Coward Soul Is Mine": *Poems of Emily Brontë* (1906).

The Victorian era (second half of the nineteenth century) yields the following list: Tennyson: for "Strong Son of God" *In Memoriam A. H. H.* (1850), and for "Crossing the Bar" *Demeter and Other Poems* (1889); Christina Rossetti: "In the Bleak Midwinter" in *The Poetical Works of Christina Georgina Rossetti* (1904), "Good Friday" in *The Prince's Progress and Other Poems* (1866), and "Up-Hill" in *Goblin-Market and Other Poems* (1862); all of the poems by Gerard Manley Hopkins: *Poems*, ed. Robert Bridges (1918); Francis Thompson, "O World Invisible": *Selected Poems of Francis Thompson* (1921).

Twentieth-century poems: Robert Frost, "A Prayer in Spring": *A Boy's Will* (London: David Nutt, 1913); T. S. Eliot's "Journey of the

Scripture Index

Person Index

Bold text indicates pages containing the individual's poetry.